DO NOT REMOVE
CARDS FROM POCKET

Maud Cuney-Hare

NORRIS WRIGHT CUNEY

AFRICAN-AMERICAN WOMEN WRITERS, 1910–1940

HENRY LOUIS GATES, JR. *General Editor*

Jennifer Burton *Associate Editor*

MAUD CUNEY-HARE

NORRIS WRIGHT CUNEY

A Tribune of the Black People

Introduction by
TERA W. HUNTER

G.K. HALL & CO.
An Imprint of Simon & Schuster Macmillan
New York

Prentice Hall International
London   Mexico City   New Delhi   Singapore   Sydney   Toronto

Introduction copyright © 1995 by Tera W. Hunter

G.K. Hall & Co.
An Imprint of Simon & Schuster Macmillan
866 Third Avenue
New York, NY 10022

Library of Congress Catalog Card Number: 94-19856

Printed in the United States of America

Printing Number
1 2 3 4 5 6 7 8 9 10

Library of Congress Cataloging-in-Publication Data
The Library of Congress has catalogued the hardcover edition of this book as follows:

Cuney-Hare, Maud, 1874–1936.
    Norris Wright Cuney : a tribune of the Black people / Maud Cuney Hare ; introduction by Tera Hunter.
    p. cm. — (African American women writers, 1910–1940)
    Originally published: New York: Crises, 1913. With new introd.
    Includes bibliographical references.
    ISBN 0-8161-1631-8 (alk. paper)
    1. Cuney, Norris Wright, 1846–1950. 2. Afro-American politicians—Texas—Biography. 3. Texas—Politics and government—1865–1950.
    I. Title. II. Series.
    E185.97.C97H3 1994
    976.4'06'092—dc20
    [B]
                                                                        94-19856
                                                                        CIP

ISBN (hardcover) 0-8161-1631-8
ISBN (paperback) 0-7838-1397-x

CONTENTS

GENERAL EDITORS' PREFACE

The past decade of our literary history might be thought of as the era of African-American women writers. Culminating in the awarding of the Pulitzer Prize to Toni Morrison and Rita Dove and the Nobel Prize for Literature to Toni Morrison in 1993, and characterized by the presence of several writers—Toni Morrison, Alice Walker, Maya Angelou, and the Delany Sisters, among others—on the *New York Times* Best Seller List, the shape of the most recent period in our literary history has been determined in large part by the writings of black women.

This, of course, has not always been the case. African-American women authors have been publishing their thoughts and feelings at least since 1773, when Phillis Wheatley published her book of poems in London, thereby bringing poetry directly to bear upon the philosophical discourse over the African's "place in nature" and his or her place in the great chain of being. The scores of words published by black women in America in the nineteenth century—most of which were published in extremely limited editions and never reprinted—have been republished in new critical editions in the forty-volume *Schomburg Library of Nineteenth-Century Black Women Writers*. The critical response to that series has led to requests from scholars and students alike for a similar series, one geared to the work by black women published between 1910 and the beginning of World War Two.

African-American Women Writers, 1910–1940 is designed to bring back into print many writers who otherwise would be unknown to contemporary readers, and to increase the availability of lesser-known texts by established writers who originally published during this critical period in African-American letters. This series implicitly acts as a chronological sequel to the Schomburg series, which focused on the origins of the black female literary tradition in America.

In less than a decade, the study of African-American women's writings has grown from its promising beginnings into a firmly established field in departments of English, American Studies, and African-American Studies. A comparison of the form and function of the original series and this sequel illustrates this dramatic shift. The *Schomburg Library* was published at the cusp of focused academic investigation into the interplay between race and gender. It covered the extensive period from the publication of Phillis Wheatley's *Poems on Various Subjects, Religious and Moral* in 1773 through the "Black Women's Era" of 1890–1910, and was designed to be an inclusive series of the major early texts by black women writers. The Schomburg Library provided a historical backdrop for black women's writings of the 1970s and 1980s, including the works of writers such as Toni Morrison, Alice Walker, Maya Angelou, and Rita Dove.

African-American Women Writers, 1910–1940 continues our effort to provide a new generation of readers access to texts—historical, sociological, and literary—that have been largely "unread" for most of this century. The series bypasses works that are important both to the period and the tradition, but that are readily available, such as Zora Neale Hurston's *Their Eyes Were Watching God*, Jessie Fauset's *Plum Bun* and *There is Confusion*, and Nella Larsen's *Quicksand* and *Passing*. Our goal is to provide access to a wide variety of rare texts. The series includes Fauset's two other novels, *The Chinaberry Tree: A Novel of American Life* and *Comedy: American Style*, and Hurston's short play, *Color Struck*, since these are not yet widely available. It also features works by virtually unknown writers, such as *A Tiny Spark*, Christina Moody's slim volume of poetry self-published in 1910, and *Reminiscences of School Life, and Hints on Teaching*, written by Fanny Jackson Coppin in the last year of her life (1913), a multi-genre work combining an autobiographical sketch and reflections on trips to England and South Africa, complete with pedagogical advice.

Cultural studies' investment in diverse resources allows the historic scope of the *African-American Women Writers* series to be more focused than the *Schomburg Library* series, which covered works written over a 137-year period. With few exceptions, the authors included in the *African-American Women Writers* series wrote their major works between 1910 and 1940. The texts reprinted include all of the works by each particular author that are not otherwise readily obtainable. As a result, two volumes contain works originally published after 1940. The Charlotte Hawkins Brown volume includes her book of etiquette published in 1941, *The Correct Thing To Do—To Say—To Wear*. One of the poetry volumes contains Maggie Pogue Johnson's *Fallen Blossoms*, published in 1951, a compilation of all her previously published and unpublished poems.

Excavational work by scholars during the past decade has been crucial to the development of *African-American Women Writers, 1910–1940*. Germinal bibliographic sources such as Anne Allen Shockley's *Afro-American Women Writers 1746–1933* and Maryemma Graham's *Database of African-American Women Writers* made the initial identification of texts possible. Other works were brought to our attention by scholars who wrote letters sharing their research. Additional texts by selected authors were then added, so that many volumes contain the complete oeuvres of particular writers. Pieces by authors without enough published work to fill an entire volume were grouped with other pieces by genre.

The two types of collections, those organized by author and those organized by genre, bring out different characteristics of black women's writings of the period. The collected works of the literary writers illustrate that many of them were experimenting with a variety of forms. Mercedes Gilbert's volume, for example, contains her 1931 collection, *Selected Gems of Poetry, Comedy, and Drama, Etc.*, as well as her 1938 novel, *Aunt Sara's Wooden God*. Georgia Douglas Johnson's volume contains her plays and short stories in addition to her poetry. Sarah Lee Brown Fleming's volume combines her 1918 novel *Hope's Highway* with her 1920 collection of poetry, *Clouds and Sunshine*.

The generic volumes both bring out the formal and thematic similarities among many of the writings and highlight the striking individuality of particular writers. Most of the plays in the volume of one-acts are social dramas whose tragic endings can be clearly attributed to miscegenation and racism. Within the context of these other plays, Marita Bonner's surrealistic theatrical vision becomes all the more striking.

The volumes of *African-American Women Writers, 1910–1940* contain reproductions of more than one hundred previously published texts, including twenty-nine plays, seventeen poetry collections, twelve novels, six autobiographies, five collections of short biographical sketches, three biographies, three histories of organizations, three black histories, two anthologies, two sociological studies, a diary, and a book of etiquette. Each volume features an introduction written by a contemporary scholar that provides crucial biographical data on each author and the historical and critical context of her work. In some cases, little information on the authors was available outside of the fragments of biographical data contained in the original introduction or in the text itself. In these instances, editors have documented the libraries and research centers where they tried to find information, in the hope that subsequent scholars will continue the necessary search to find the "lost" clues to the women's stories in the rich stores of papers, letters, photographs, and other primary materials scattered throughout the country that have yet to be fully catalogued.

Many of the thrilling moments that occurred during the development of this series were the result of previously fragmented pieces of these women's histories suddenly coming together, such as Adele Alexander's uncovering of an old family photograph, picturing her own aunt with Addie Hunton, the author Alexander was researching. Claudia Tate's examination of Georgia Douglas Johnson's papers in the Moorland-Spingarn Research Center of Howard University resulted in the discovery of a wealth of previously unpublished work.

The slippery quality of race itself emerged during the construction of the series. One of the short novels originally intended for inclusion in the series had to be cut when the family of the author protested that the writer was not of African descent. Another case involved Louise Kennedy's sociological study *The Negro Peasant Turns Inward*. The fact that none of the available biographical material on Kennedy specifically mentioned race, combined with some coded criticism in a review in the *Crisis*, convinced editor Sheila Smith McCoy that Kennedy was probably white.

These women, taken together, begin to chart the true vitality, and complexity, of the literary tradition that African-American women have generated, using a wide variety of forms. They testify to the fact that the monumental works of Hurston, Larsen, and Fauset, for example, emerged out of a larger cultural context; they were not exceptions or aberrations. Indeed, their contributions to American literature and culture, as this series makes clear, were fundamental not only to the shaping of the African-American tradition but to the American tradition as well.

Henry Louis Gates, Jr.
Jennifer Burton

PUBLISHER'S NOTE

In the *African-American Women Writers, 1910-1940* series, G.K. Hall not only is making available previously neglected works that, in many cases, have been long out of print; we are also, whenever possible, publishing these works in facsimiles reprinted from their original editions including, when available, reproductions of original title pages, copyright pages, and photographs.

When it was not possible for us to reproduce a complete facsimile edition of a particular work (for example, if the original exists only as a handwritten draft or is too fragile to be reproduced), we have attempted to preserve the essence of the original by resetting the work exactly as it originally appeared. Therefore, any typographical errors, strikeouts, or other anomalies reflect our efforts to give the reader a true sense of the original work.

We trust that these facsimile and reprint editions, together with the new introductory essays, will be both useful and historically enlightening to scholars and students alike.

INTRODUCTION

BY TERA W. HUNTER

Maud Cuney-Hare* lent her considerable expertise and resources to carving out a place for African Americans in music and in community theaters. In 1927, she worked to establish the Allied Arts Center in downtown Boston on behalf of the League of Women for Community Services. She wrote a letter to her friend Adelaide Casely Hayford regarding her plans: "If I am fortunate in securing this place, it will mean that I can put our young folks' talent and wares in a section that will be in the regular stream irrespective of race. I abhor the segregated districts."[1] This letter is both telling and ironic in articulating the ambitions of a multitalented woman whose own life transcended many of the limits imposed upon members of her race and sex. The biography of her father, which she published in 1913, offers some insight into the family's history, but its focus on the famous politician, businessman, and labor leader necessarily minimizes what we can learn from it about the author's own extraordinary life. A full study of the concert pianist, musicologist, playwright, and anthologist awaits scholarly attention, but in the meantime we can piece together a few fascinating remnants of her past from disparate sources.

Maud Cuney-Hare's life extended from the tumultuous period of Reconstruction through the hard times of the Great Depression. She was born 16 February 1874 and raised on the island city of Galveston, Texas; she died of cancer in Boston, Massachusetts, shortly before her sixtieth birthday. She grew up in a loving family that was able to provide her and a younger brother, Lloyd

Garrison, with all the necessities of life and many luxuries unavailable to average Americans of the time, black or white. Both of her parents, Adeline Dowdy Cuney, originally from Mississippi, and Norris Wright Cuney, a native of Texas, were the acknowledged mulatto offspring of white planters and slave women. Both benefited from formal educations and lives of relative ease as a result of their paternity.

It is not surprising that Cuney-Hare would devote her life to the arts, especially to music and literature, given her background. Both parents were gifted artists; her mother was a beautiful soprano who performed publicly before her marriage, and her father played bass violin as a youngster, having learned the art from an elderly slave. The mellifluous sounds of singing and musical instruments pervaded the Cuney home. Even during distressful periods, music helped to alleviate the family's encounters with the harsh reprisals that resulted from her father's labor and political activities.[2] Literature was also regularly enjoyed in the Cuney household, especially by Maud's father, who shared his fondness for great Western poets and writers by reading aloud and reciting verses to his children.

After graduating from Central High School in 1890, Maud Cuney left Texas and entered the dual world of a prestigious, predominantly white institution and a social and intellectual circle of elite black Bostonians. She studied pianoforte at the New England Conservatory of Music, and later studied English literature at Harvard University's Lowell Institute.[3] At the conservatory she and Florida Desverney, the daughter of a prosperous cotton dealer in Savannah, Georgia, were the only students of African descent and they encountered racial prejudice shortly after their arrival. Their white classmates objected to living in a dormitory with blacks, but, true to the tenacious Cuney blood that flowed through her veins, Maud refused to yield to pressure from the school's administrators to find off-campus housing.[4] When she later spoke to her friend Casely Hayford of abhorring segregation, it was this bitter episode that was imprinted on her memory. After completing her courses at the conservatory, she took private lessons from Emil Ludwig, a pupil of Anton Rubinstein, and from Edwin Klahre, a protégé of Franz Liszt.

School did not consume all of Cuney's energy during her years in Boston. She was an integral part of the Charles Street Circle (or "West End Set"), presided over by Josephine St. Pierre Ruffin, a woman's rights activist and the widow of George Lewis Ruffin, a prominent attorney and judge. The Ruffins' magisterial home provided a gathering place for free-born aristocrats of color.[5] Intimate afternoons and evenings of classical European music and oratory provided the opportunity to make the acquaintance of peers from the surrounding city. One gentleman in particular, the handsome and gifted W. E. B. Du Bois, caught Maud Cuney's attention upon their arrival in Cambridge at about the same time. "She reigned in Colored Boston, with me among the hosts of young men bowing before her throne," Du Bois later acknowledged.[6] His adoration of her beauty was obvious even in the last decade of his nearly century-long life; he remembered her as a "tall, imperious brunette, with gold-bronze skin, brilliant eyes and coils of black hair" (Du Bois, 124). The young scholars fell in love and became engaged, but never married. Each ultimately chose another spouse. According to Du Bois's most recent biographer, their mutual affection apparently endured, however, and they "would remain much more than friends" until her death (Lewis, 104–6, 116).

In 1897, Maud Cuney returned to Texas to serve as the director of music at the Deaf, Dumb, and Blind Institute for Colored Youth in Austin, a school that her father had been instrumental in founding. A year later she entered into a strained and short-lived marriage with J. Frank McKinley, a Chicago physician, who was at least two decades her senior. At the insistence of Dr. McKinley, the newlyweds took advantage of their Caucasian heritage and features and passed as "Spanish-Americans." Their fictive Latin pedigree received official sanction on their daughter Vera's birth certificate. But these and other tactics to evade segregation were the source of marital discord, publicly exposed during an intense custody battle upon the couple's divorce in 1904 (Gatewood, 176; *Guardian*).

Maud's conflict with her husband over the issue of "passing" is thrown into greater relief by a passage in her father's biography describing an occasion just a few years before her wedding when a white restaurant cashier in New York presumed she was a

"Spanish girl-bride." In response, Cuney proudly declared her true racial identity and refused any other designation. When she reported the encounter to her father, he heartily approved of her rejoinder. She explained his opinion: "He abhorred above all things the supposedly easier way of 'passing for white,' and instilled in my young brother and me a hatred and contempt for the cowardly method which is upheld by many who can successfully disown their Negro blood" (*Cuney*, 154). The biography made no mention of her own brief and embarrassing interlude on the other side of the color line six years later. In fact, the unhappy marriage seems to have receded into obscurity after it ended, almost as if it never occurred. Nor did she expose in the book other paternal relatives who had passed for white, including her aunts, Jennie and Laura, and her cousin Mae, daughter of her uncle Nelson.[7]

Despite the equivocation that troubled her first marriage, Maud Cuney McKinley did not entirely repudiate her upbringing by a family that consciously identified itself with the struggles of black people. She followed the example of her mother's commitment to "racial uplift" by teaching piano in the social service settlement program at the Institutional African Methodist Episcopal Church in Chicago from 1900 to 1901.[8] Though it is unclear whether she and her husband were separated at the time, by 1903 she had returned to Texas, where she taught music at Prairie View Agricultural and Mechanical College, another black institution that benefited from her father's support. A year later Maud moved again, presumably with her toddler daughter in tow, this time back to Boston, where she launched a career as a concert pianist and private instructor. On 10 August 1904 she gave marriage a second try, this time with William Parker Hare, the scion from an old-line black Boston family.[9] Their marriage lasted until her death.

Over the next three decades, Maud Cuney-Hare's talents would blossom in full. In 1918, five years after the publication of her father's biography, she edited and published a collection of poetry, *The Message of the Trees*. She dedicated the book to the memory of her daughter, Vera, who had died unexpectedly a decade earlier, but in many ways it paid homage to her father's intellectual inspiration. The anthology, largely ignored in African-American literary history, contained over one hundred poems on the subject of trees, all by white authors, with the exception of Paul Lawrence Dunbar.[10] A decade later, she wrote and produced *Antar of Araby*, a four-act romantic drama, which was the first play by an African American that introduced a foreign character. This time race took center stage: the protagonist, an Arabian warrior and poet, was depicted as a despised black slave struggling to win respect and overcome the barriers of bigotry. Cuney-Hare produced this play and others by African-American writers at the Musical Art Studio she helped establish in Boston (Shockley, 336).

Although the literary and dramatic arts would remain important to Cuney-Hare, music was not only the focus of her professional training, but also her first love. By the 1920s she had become well known throughout the North as a pianist and lecturer. She performed at such institutions as the Brooklyn Academy of Music, Syracuse University, the Albany Historical and Art Association, and the Harvard Musical Association.[11] Her longest-running artistic liaison was with William Howard Richardson, a baritone who also appeared with the Roland Hayes trio. They performed together from around 1913 until the early 1930s in concert halls throughout the nation and abroad (*Musicians*, 313, 353, 364–67).

As a pianist, playwright, and producer, Cuney-Hare was undoubtedly very able, but the most tangible gift she bequeathed to future generations was her intellectual musings on the history of African-American music. Like the anthropologist Zora Neale Hurston, her younger contemporary, Cuney-Hare was very interested in the African roots of blacks in the New World. She traveled to the Virgin Islands, Puerto Rico, Cuba, Mexico, Haiti, and Louisiana in search of African cultural continuities evident in the music and dances of the Americas. She traced African bodily aesthetics in the tango of Argentina, the habanera of Cuba, and the bamboula of Louisiana. She wrote about the cross-fertilization of Anglo and African cultures in the work songs of black seafaring laborers and longshoremen on the docks of Galveston, New Orleans, and Baltimore—no doubt influenced by her father's work as a boatman in his youth and as a stevedore later in life. Cuney-Hare also undertook research about great musicians of Negro heritage, from the German violinist George Polgren Bridgetower, protégé of Beethoven, to American singers Paul Robeson and E. Azalia Hackley and pioneers of vaudeville and minstrelsy Anna Madah Hyer and Emma Louise Hyer. She published her interpretative findings in journals and magazines such as the *Crisis*, for which she served as musical editor, *Musical Quarterly*, the *Christian Science Monitor*, the *Musical Observer*, and *Musical America*. Through her research and travels she amassed a large private collection of sheet music and colored lithographs chronicling over a hundred years of music history, which she exhibited in Boston at the William Richardson Vocal Studio, in New Haven, Connecticut, at the public library, and in other venues nationwide.[12] Most importantly, years of thoughtful research culminated in a major study published shortly after her death, *Negro Musicians and Their Music*, which was dedicated to her musical partner, William Richardson. The book and her earlier writings originated during one of the most important literary and artistic movements of black Americans, the Harlem Renaissance of the 1920s and 1930s.

Comments by one of the leading writers of this "New Negro" movement suggest that her magnum opus may not have received widespread attention at the time of its publication. In 1944 Langston Hughes bemoaned the absence of a book on African-American music written by a black author, thereby overlooking Cuney-Hare's important work.[13] Similar oversights will continue until her study has received the scholarly recognition and critical treatment it so richly deserves. When given full consideration, Cuney-Hare's investigation of New World cultures arisen from the African Diaspora will be praised for its pioneering and insightful contributions to American cultural history.

If the life and writings of Maud Cuney-Hare have been insufficiently acknowledged, so too have her father's.[14] *Norris Wright Cuney: A Tribune of the Black People*, is the most comprehensive study to date of one of the most important political leaders in the late-nineteenth-century South. From 1883 until his downfall in

1896, Cuney was the leader of the Republican party in Texas and a pivotal player at the national level as well. Largely laudatory and uncritical, Cuney-Hare's biography of her father is constructed in the great-men-in-history tradition. The work is based, however, on a wide range of sources, including personal and business correspondence, newspaper articles, official records, and the author's own recollections. Scholars of Texas, Southern, political, labor, and African-American histories have cited the study widely.

Norris Wright Cuney, in many respects, was an archetypal member of an elite group of African-American slaves. In comparison to most mulatto children, who were the products of sexual exploitation, he grew up privileged. His father, Philip W. Cuney, was among the top 54 slaveholders in Texas on the basis of number of slaves owned. His Sunnyville Plantation near Hempstead, devoted to cotton and dairy farming, included 2,000 acres of land and 105 slaves.[15] He had a long-standing relationship with Adeline Stuart, his head house slave, which lasted through his second and third legal marriages. Stuart gave birth to eight children, of whom Norris Wright Cuney, born in 1846, was the fourth. Shortly after moving with his black family to Houston in 1853, Philip Cuney manumitted two of his sons, Joseph and Nelson, and sent them off to the Wylie Street School in Pittsburgh, Pennsylvania, headed by George Vashon, a distinguished black educator. In 1859, at the age of thirteen, Norris Wright would follow his brothers to Vashon's school, where he learned to read. By 1860 his sister Jennie was studying at Madame Nichol's Institute for Young Ladies in Germany and the remaining members of the African branch of the family tree had been freed as well (Woodson, 123). During the Civil War, Philip Cuney became a general for the Confederacy, and his son Joseph a soldier for the Union—a striking image of the divided loyalties of interracial Southern families at mid-century.

Aside from the education Norris Wright received while living in the North, one other experience would have a lasting impact on his life. Cut off from his father's resources and at least one brother's companionship during the war, he quit school and became a boatman on the *Grey Eagle*, which traveled the Mississippi River to such cities as Cincinnati, St. Louis, and New Orleans. His excursions would prepare him for his later occupation as a steve-dore, but they also exposed him to the world of politics. He met such men as P. B. S. Pinchback, the future lieutenant governor of Louisiana, and George T. Ruby, later the president of the Union League in Texas and a state senator. Not much is known about his actual relationships with these political leaders, but Ruby's influence would become apparent by the end of the war.

Cuney moved to Galveston in 1865 to assist Ruby in building the Union League, the grass-roots precursor of the Republican party. How he maintained himself and, after 1871, a wife and two children, is an enigma explained only by speculation. We know that in 1872 he was the inspector of customs in Galveston. In 1875 and perhaps 1876 he ran a liquor and tobacco business; he was twice arrested by the U.S. Marshal for violating internal revenue laws. But before 1872 and between 1877 and 1881 Cuney had little or no visible means of support. Galveston city directories for the latter period list no occupation under his name. Cuney-Hare does not mention her father's liquor business and arrests. She also offers no explanation for the gaps in his employment history, nor does she repeat the conjectures of others. According to some sources, his income derived from involvement with a gambling and whiskey ring known as the "Belle Poole Establishment," which had its headquarters near the customshouse. Moreover, the ring allegedly swindled the paltry wages of black workers.[16]

If Cuney was guilty of such corruption, he undermined the Union League's objective—to empower ex-slaves to use their collective strength to counter the unscrupulous practices of ex-masters. Black political activism was difficult enough in the uncharted waters of the town and the state without the added burden of a tarnished character. The constraints upon black political participation were enormous in Texas, where emancipation arrived several months later than elsewhere, delayed by the state's isolation from the forces of war and social transformation. No black man served in a major executive or judicial office in Texas during Reconstruction, and only fourteen held seats in the state legislature, including two in the senate—the highest office achieved. African Americans formed the majority of the Republican party, which was top-heavy with an elite white leadership more interested in reconciling with former Confederates and building railroads than in promoting justice for ex-slaves.[17]

How Cuney climbed the Republican party hierarchy under these circumstances was essential to his longevity on the political scene. In 1870 Cuney received his first governmental appointment, as the assistant sergeant-at-arms in the state legislature, in gratitude for successfully galvanizing black Texans to elect Edmund J. Davis as governor. A year later he returned home and became president of a newly organized Union League chapter, thereby preparing himself to become the foremost black Republican in the state after Ruby moved to New Orleans in the early 1870s (Hinze, 11–14; Rice, 35–36). Both positions demonstrate the shrewd double-pronged strategy that would structure Cuney's entire career: he pursued power within the white-dominated infrastructure as well as through autonomous black institutions. From 1872 until 1896 he was a delegate to every national convention of his party, which increased both his stature in the state and his visibility in the nation. As an alderman in Galveston in the early 1880s, the only elected public position he ever held, he represented a predominantly white ward. Many local whites loved him, and many of his adversaries at least respected him. Meanwhile, Cuney created a constituency by unionizing waterfront workers, attending regional and national black-led conventions, and associating with one of the most well known fraternal orders, the Masons. Black voters generally stood with him, though they sometimes were ahead of his political thought and felt stymied by his ties to the white establishment.

The definitive turning point that staked out Cuney's post at the helm of the state Republican party occurred in 1883 and 1884. The death of Governor Davis in 1883, the party's nominal chief, gave Cuney the recognition he had earned as the actual leader of the majority. His command over peers within the national convention garnered for him the vice presidency of the convention in 1884. That same year his ability to deliver the votes of his delegation to James G. Blaine, the eventual nominee for president, made him the undisputed party man of the state. His election as Texas's national committeeman the following year confirmed his authority. At the national convention in 1888, he campaigned for Benjamin

Harrison as he had for Blaine. Harrison's ensuing election to the presidency resulted in Cuney's most eminent appointment, collector of customs at Galveston, then the most important federal assignment ever bestowed on a black Southerner. The collectorship granted him the power to dole out federal patronage and largesse to Texans—eagerly solicited by blacks and whites alike. He served in this position from 1889 until 1893, when Harrison was defeated.

Cuney's enhanced authority also stiffened the resolve of white dissidents within the ranks of the Texas Republican party, who labeled him a panjandrum and named themselves the "Lily" Republicans. He returned the favor with the moniker "Lily whites." The Lilies were especially strong in Texas, though they were part of a region-wide movement determined to eradicate black political influence. Cuney was able to stave off his foes initially, but he suffered from the protracted struggle and a round of other defeats between 1893 and 1896. In 1893 he was removed from his position as collector of customs, and whites were then less obliged to accede to his demands. Three years later he lost his seat as the national committeeman for Texas, as well as important battles in the state and national conventions. His political career was brought to a halt in 1896, the year following his wife's death.[18]

Cuney's public career had lasted a remarkably long time, particularly since the political fortunes of blacks were decidedly bleak after 1877. His ascent, ironically, had paralleled the demise of the Radical Republicans, the liberal wing of the party who were in control during Reconstruction, and the victory of the Redeemers, a group of extremely reactionary white Southerners hurled into power through Ku Klux Klan violence, fraud, and intimidation. As the moderate Northern rulers of the Republican party turned away from protecting black political rights in the South, the Democrats were given the tacit nod to reassert their hegemony below the Mason-Dixon line. The rise of the Lily whites symbolized white Southern Republican refusal to coalesce with a black majority articulating an iota of independent will. Cuney's engaging and effective political life during this period is a tribute to the resiliency of a people who continued to participate in electoral politics despite the increasingly overwhelming odds against them. His downfall in 1896 and his death in 1898 coincided with the rise of de jure disfranchisement of African Americans at century's end.

No account of Cuney's political activities is complete without an understanding of his role in the labor movement. His diverse job résumé was extremely unusual in the Lone Star State at a time when most blacks were concentrated in either farm work or domestic service. Relative to its population, Texas had the lowest proportion of black wage earners in areas outside agriculture of any state, in part because of the small number of antebellum slave artisans and also because of lagging industrialization and urbanization. The growth of such transportation enterprises as railroad construction and shipping in the 1870s began to open up opportunities for black men as porters, maintenance workers, and, eventually, dock workers. African-American men excluded from the white longshoremen's union founded in 1869 initiated their own Longshoremen's Benevolent Association a year later, but they were still effectively locked out of waterfront jobs by the white monopoly.[19]

Cuney may have been an organizer of this association, the city's first black labor union, but his relationship to the union movement was marked by ambivalence, as the Great Strike of 1877 illustrates. Railroad workers in Martinsburg, West Virginia, walked off their jobs in the heat of the summer in protest of wage cuts, high unemployment, and exorbitant profits for stockholders. Their insurgency stimulated a domino effect of spontaneous walkouts that left few territories in the nation untouched and accumulated sympathy from laborers in other fields along the way. The federal government sided with the owners and sent out the militia, just recently recalled from protecting ex-slaves in the South. The result was a bloody and epochal moment of class strife—the first national strike.[20]

Just as the strike passed its climax, black and a few white common laborers in Galveston caught the contagion of rebellion.[21] Several hundred male laborers from the wharves, mills, construction trades, and railroads gathered in a boisterous street parade, demanding wages of two dollars a day and renouncing further wage cuts. Meanwhile, black women, who mostly worked as laundresses, cooks, child-nurses,[22] and maids, organized a strike of their own.

Norris Wright Cuney intervened at one of the men's public rallies, denouncing the laborers for "creating all sorts of discord and stirring up all sorts of bad blood." Ignoring the police brutality that left one striker wounded by gunfire, Cuney chastised the strikers and entreated them to return home to their wives and children, for they were "guilty in a vain attempt to revolutionize the industrial interests of the city."[23]

Cuney's conciliatory attitude toward the white businessmen further elevated him in their estimation, but his standing among ordinary citizens plummeted. The domestic workers, calling themselves the Ladies of Labor, criticized their brothers for granting a platform to a turncoat, though they saved their strongest vehemence for employers and for Cuney himself. "I emphatically say that by such leaders for the last twelve years we have been bought out and sold out," declared one domestic worker. Other black women joined in the chorus castigating Cuney for "stealing" their rights and daring him to repeat his acquiescent speech to their faces. Despite Cuney's cooperation with employers' and municipal officials' efforts to strangle the protests, the workers secured some concessions in the end.[24]

Maud Cuney-Hare's construction of this event blurred the line between her roles as a detached reporter and an adoring daughter. Her unwavering faith in her father prompted a portrait that praised his display of courage and integrity in the face of an angry mob whose grievances "were not important enough to demand public sympathy" (*Cuney*, 24). Neither Cuney at the time nor his daughter in hindsight recognized how much he was out of step with the masses' fundamental demands for respect and fair remuneration. His infamous speech, however, would have more contradictory consequences for the future of black labor.

In business as in politics, 1883 was a milestone year for Cuney. In a shrewd move that both benefited his own financial situation and enhanced the livelihood of Galveston's black male workers, Cuney became a stevedore, the intermediary responsible for hiring out longshoremen (unskilled workers who loaded and unloaded cargo) and screwmen (skilled workers who compressed and packed cotton bales in the holds of ships using jack screws). After several failed attempts, he finally procured a contract for black longshoremen on the Mallory wharf. He did so by bolstering his corps with men recruited from New Orleans and by slightly underbidding the wages of whites.[25] No doubt, his criticism of the 1877 strike now literally paid off.

Cuney next moved to organize the Colored Screwmen's Association, invested money in tools and training, and notified William L. Moody, president of the Galveston Cotton Exchange, of the availability of this new pool of skilled workers. Galveston ranked third in the world in cotton exports in the 1870s, and the white screwmen's union often fell short in supplying enough men at the height of the season. The port city's capacity to advance its economic development depended on its ability to broaden its search for skilled labor, Cuney argued.[26] Moody and his associates grasped the familiar correlation between prosperity and the use of black labor, but their working-class counterparts balked. When the first contract took effect in April, white screwmen walked out until the end of August to protest the employment of black men. But in the end, they lost not only the battle against Cuney, but also the war to maintain exclusive control over their trade.[27]

African-American dock workers continued to make gains under Cuney's leadership, and his business as a stevedore became lucrative. In 1884, the Trades Assembly of Galveston opened its membership to black unions for the first time, which did nothing if not inflame the animosity of white waterfront workers who steadfastly refused to unite across the color line. Tensions came to a head once again the following year, when white longshoremen struck against the Mallory Steamship Company and Cuney supplied blacks to take their place. Black laborers were able to maintain a strong position on Galveston's major wharves when the strike ended.[28] But the benefits gained from continual racial conflict ultimately accrued to the shippers, for as long as blacks and whites remained divided they were too weak to effectively challenge the power of the shipping company owners.

Was Cuney a labor organizer or a businessman? Did he stand for the interests of labor or capital? Despite his refusal to stand behind the working class in 1877, Cuney found a way to reconcile his personal ambitions for financial aggrandizement through the free enterprise system with the creation of opportunities for other African Americans. He functioned in the labor movement much as he strategized in electoral politics—with a double vision. He simultaneously attained the confidence of white businessmen by supplying them with surplus labor and won the respect of black men by creating jobs for them. Black male workers, in turn, formed his political constituency, which gave him leverage in the Republican party—as long as their votes counted.

Cuney often assumed the mantle of spokesman for his race, but his views were not always consistent with those of the majority. He opposed the Kansas exodus of 1879, in which blacks left Texas en masse both to escape debt peonage, high rent, disfranchisement, rape, and violence, and to entitle themselves to land, education, and the pursuit of their basic human and civil rights.[29] In the 1890s, when many blacks were joining the radical agrarian Populist party, Cuney remained loyal to the passé moderate Republicans. He considered the ideas of the Populists too far removed from capitalism and too intimate with socialism and communism, though he modified his views at the eleventh hour of his tenure, when fusing with the Populists offered the last hope of political survival (Rice, 68–85; *Cuney*, 159).

Cuney's opposition to Populism and the Kansas exodus may be attributed to his city roots and his devotion to an urban agenda. The strongest adherents of agrarian reform and the sources of the greatest upsurge to emigrate came from rural areas, where most African Americans lived and suffered. On the other hand, Cuney's influence was much broader than the confines of his hometown, and he rarely, if ever, resisted speaking as a representative of the whole black race. His social background, his views on a variety of social issues, his faith in the system—in these and other respects, Cuney fit the profile of most black leaders of his time.[30]

Cuney also championed many measures with broad appeal. His commitment to improving the quality and quantity of public education stands out in particular. He believed that school segregation "brands the colored race as an inferior one," a position that resembled the conclusion drawn by the Supreme Court in the landmark *Brown v. Board of Education of Topeka* decision in 1954 (*Cuney*, 38). Similarly, he strongly condemned lynching and mob violence. He openly criticized Southern governors who were eager to ban interracial prizefighting in the ring, but who were apathetic and reticent in using force to stop race riots against blacks on the streets (*Cuney*, 103).

Neither this short essay nor Maud Cuney-Hare's more thorough book can do justice to Norris Wright Cuney's complex and rich life. We can only hope that this reprint edition will inspire other scholars to do further research.

NOTES

*In accordance with her practice later on in life, I have hyphenated Maud Cuney-Hare's name throughout this essay. I would like to thank Marya McQuirter for her research assistance and Leslie Rowland for her comments.

[1]Cuney-Hare to Mrs. [Adelaide Casely] Hayford, 25 September 1927, as quoted in Adelaide M. Cromwell, *An African Victorian Feminist: The Life and Times of Adelaide Smith Casely Hayford, 1868–1960* (London: Frank Cass and Co., 1986), 131.

[2]See Cuney-Hare, *Norris Wright Cuney: A Tribune of the Black People* (1913; facsimile reprint, Austin, Tex.: Seck-Vaughn, 1968), 46; hereafter cited as *Cuney*. Page numbers refer to this facsimile of the original, a facsimile of which is published in the present volume.

[3]Frank Lincoln Mather, ed., *Who's Who of the Colored Race* (Chicago: n.p., 1915), 129; hereafter cited in text.

[4]See *Cuney*, 131–34. Black students at Harvard University also rallied to her defense. See *The Autobiography of W. E. B. Du Bois; a Soliloquy on Viewing My Life from the Last Decade of Its First Century* (New York: International Publishers, 1968), 124; Willard B. Gatewood, *Aristocrats of Color: The Black Elite, 1880–1920* (Bloomington: Indiana University Press, 1990), 267. Both of these works are hereafter cited in text.

[5]David Levering Lewis, *W. E. B. Du Bois: Biography of a Race, 1868–1919* (New York: Henry Holt and Co., 1993), 104–6; Gatewood, 109–13. Lewis is hereafter cited in text.

[6]Boston *Guardian*, 15 April 1936, in Schomburg Center for Black Culture, Clipping File (microfilm); hereafter cited in text as *Guardian*.

[7]C[arter] G. Woodson, "The Cuney Family," *Negro History Bulletin* 11 (March 1948): 124; hereafter cited in text.

[8]Mather, 129; James R. Grossman, *Land of Hope: Chicago, Black Southerners and the Great Migration* (Chicago: University of Chicago Press, 1989), 140.

[9]Not much is known about the second marriage either. Some sources

have identified 1906 as the year the couple married. I have relied on Mather, 129, and Lorraine Roses and Ruth Elizabeth Randolph, *Harlem Renaissance and Beyond: Literary Biographies of 100 Black Women Writers, 1900–1945* (Boston: G. K. Hall and Co., 1990), 148; Roses and Randolph hereafter cited in text.

[10]Ann Allen Shockley, ed., *Afro-American Women Writers, 1746–1933: An Anthology and Critical Guide* (Boston: G. K. Hall and Co., 1988), 336; hereafter cited in text.

[11]Cuney-Hare, *Negro Musicians and Their Music* (Washington, D.C.: Associated Publishers, 1936), xi; Roses and Randolph, 149. The Cuney-Hare work is hereafter cited in text as *Musicians*.

[12]*Crisis* (July 1934): 203; *Norfolk Journal and Guide*, 6 April 1935, in Schomburg Center for Black Culture, Clipping File.

[13]Jon Michael Spencer, *Blues and Evil* (Knoxville: University of Kentucky Press, 1993), xi.

[14]See the only known publication by Norris Wright Cuney, "A Tribute to Haïtien Heroism," Afterword to *Dessalines, a Dramatic Tale: A Single Chapter from Haiti's History*, by William Edgar Easton (Galveston, Tex.: J. W. Burson Co., 1893), 122–28.

[15]Virginia Neal Hinze, "Norris Wright Cuney," Master's thesis, Rice University, 1965, 3; hereafter cited in text.

[16]Hinze, 14–15; Lawrence Rice, *The Negro in Texas, 1874–1900* (Baton Rouge: Louisiana University Press, 1971), 37. Rice hereafter cited in text.

[17]Alwyn Barr, "Black Legislators of Reconstruction Texas," *Civil War History* 32 (December 1986): 340–52; James Alex Baggett, "Origins of Early Texas Republican Party Leadership," *Journal of Southern History* 40 (August 1974): 441–54; Carl Moneyhon, *Republicanism in Texas* (Austin: University of Texas Press, 1980), 82–137; Eric Foner, *Reconstruction: America's Unfinished Revolution, 1863–1877* (New York: Oxford University Press, 1988), 307.

[18]Hinze, 54–131; Rice, 34–52; Paul Douglas Casdorph, "Norris Wright Cuney and Texas Republican Politics, 1883–1896," *Southwestern Historical Quarterly* 67 (April 1965): 455–64.

[19]Rice, 184–90; Alwyn Barr, *Black Texans: A History of Negroes in Texas, 1528–1971* (Austin, Tex.: Jenkins Publishing Co., 1973), 92–93.

[20]Philip S. Foner, *The Great Labor Uprising of 1877* (New York: Monad Press, 1977).

[21]Cuney-Hare erroneously dates the strike as having occurred in 1876. See *Cuney*, 23–26.

[22]*Child-nurses* was the term used for nannies during this period.

[23]*Galveston Daily News*, 1 August 1877.

[24]*Galveston Daily News*, 7 August 1877; Philip S. Foner and Ronald L. Lewis, eds., *The Black Worker: A Documentary History from Colonial Times to the Present*, vol. 2 (Philadelphia: Temple University Press, 1978), 167; Tera W. Hunter, "Household Workers in the Making: Afro-American Women in Atlanta and the New South, 1861 to 1920," Ph.D. diss., Yale University, 1990, 152–62; Hinze, 24.

[25]James V. Reese, "The Evolution of an Early Texas Union: The Screwmen's Benevolent Association of Galveston, 1866–1891," *Southwestern Historical Quarterly* 85 (October 1971): 179–85; hereafter cited in text.

[26]*Galveston Daily News*, 16 March 1883; Reese, 179–85; Gary Cartwright, *Galveston: A History of the Island* (New York: Atheneum, 1991), 117.

[27]Cuney-Hare confused the screwmen's strike of 1883 and the long-shoremen's strike of 1885. Her description of the 1883 strike fits some of the details of the 1885 event. See *Cuney*, 42–47. The most reliable account of the 1883 strike is Reese, 169, 179–85. For information on the 1885 strike, see Kenneth Kann, "The Knights of Labor and the Southern Black Worker," *Labor History* 18 (Winter 1977): 56–57; and Hinze, 27–33. Kann hereafter cited in text.

[28]Kann, 56–57; and Hinze, 27–33. For an example of Cuney supplying strikebreakers to New Orleans, see Eric Arneson, *Waterfront Workers of New Orleans: Race, Class, and Politics, 1863–1923* (New York: Oxford University Press, 1991), 139, 300.

[29]See "Resolution from the National Conference of Colored Men, Nashville, 1875," in Herbert Aptheker, ed., *A Documentary History of the Negro People in the United States*, vol. 2 (New York: Citadel, 1966), 723–24; Rice, 198–204; *Cuney*, 30–31.

[30]For more on black leadership, see Thomas Holt, *Black over White: Negro Political Leadership in South Carolina during Reconstruction* (Urbana: University of Illinois Press, 1977).

BIBLIOGRAPHY

PRIMARY SOURCES

SELECTED PUBLICATIONS BY MAUD CUNEY-HARE

"Afro-American Folk Song Contributions." *Musical Observer* 15 (February 1917): 13, 21, 51.

Antar of Araby. In *Plays and Pageants from the Life of the Negro*, edited by Willis Richardson. Washington, D.C.: Associated Publishers, 1930.

"Antar, Negro Poet of Arabia." *Crisis* (June 1924): 64–66; (July 1924): 117–19.

"Ethiopian Art." *Crisis* (October 1921): 259.

"Folk Music of the Creoles" and "Negro Music in Porto Rico." In *Negro: An Anthology*, edited by Nancy Cunard. London: Wishart & Co., 1934; New York: Negro Universities Press, 1969.

"George Polgren Bridgetower." *Crisis* (June 1927): 122, 137.

"History and Song in the Virgin Islands: The Latest Gift of Folk Music to the United States." *Crisis* (April 1933): 83–84; (May 1933): 108, 118.

"Mabed Ibn Ouhab." *Crisis* (April 1925): 258–60.

The Message of the Trees: An Anthology of Leaves and Branches. Boston: Cornhill Company, 1918.

Negro Musicians and Their Music. Washington, D.C.: Associated Publishers, 1936.

"A Revival of Chantey Singing." *Christian Science Monitor* (21 June 1924): 7.

Six Creole Songs with Original Creole and Translated English Text. New York: Carl Fischer, 1921.

"Three Men Who Spread the Fame of the Creole." *Christian Science Monitor* (8 June 1924): 7.

OTHER PRIMARY SOURCES

Aptheker, Herbert, ed. *A Documentary History of the Negro People in the United States.* 3 vols. New York: Citadel, 1951–73.

Cuney, Norris Wright." A Tribute to Haïtien Heroism." Afterword to *Dessalines, a Dramatic Tale: A Single Chapter from Haiti's History*, by William Edgar Easton. Galveston, Tex.: J. W. Burson Co., 1893.

Du Bois, W. E. B. *The Autobiography of W. E. B. Du Bois: A Soliloquy on Viewing My Life from the Last Decade of Its First Century.* New York: International Publishers, 1968.

Foner, Philip S., and Ronald L. Lewis, eds. *The Black Worker: A Documentary History from Colonial Times to the Present.* 8 vols. Philadelphia: Temple University Press, 1978–84.

Galveston Daily News, August 1877.

Clipping File, Schomburg Center for Black Culture (microfilm).

SECONDARY SOURCES

Allen, Ruth. *Chapters in the History of Organized Labor in Texas.* Austin: University of Texas Press, 1941.

Arneson, Eric. *Waterfront Workers of New Orleans: Race, Class, and Politics, 1863–1923.* New York: Oxford University Press, 1991.

Baggett, James Alex. "Origins of Early Texas Republican Party Leadership." *Journal of Southern History* 40 (August 1974): 441–54.

Barr, Alwyn. *Black Texans: A History of Negroes in Texas, 1528–1971.* Austin, Tex.: Jenkins Publishing Co., 1973.

———. "Black Legislators of Reconstruction Texas." *Civil War History* 34 (December 1986): 340–51.

Cartwright, Gary. *Galveston: A History of the Island.* New York: Atheneum, 1991.

Casdorph, Paul Douglas. "Norris Wright Cuney and Texas Republican Politics, 1883–1896." *Southwestern Historical Quarterly* 67 (April 1965): 455–64.

Cromwell, Adelaide M. *An African Victorian Feminist: The Life and Times of Adelaide Smith Casely Hayford.* London: Frank Cass and Co., 1986.

Foner, Eric. *Freedom's Lawmakers: A Directory of Black Officeholders during Reconstruction.* New York: Oxford University Press, 1993.

———. *Reconstruction: America's Unfinished Revolution,1863–1877.* New York: Harper and Row, 1988.

Foner, Philip S. *The Great Labor Uprising of 1877.* New York: Monad Press, 1977.

Gatewood, Willard B. *Aristocrats of Color: The Black Elite, 1880–1920.* Bloomington: Indiana University Press, 1993.

Grossman, James R. *Land of Hope: Chicago, Black Southerners and the Great Migration.* Chicago: University of Chicago Press, 1989.

Hine, Darlene Clark, Elsa Barkley Brown, and Rosalyn Terborg-Penn, eds. *Black Women in America: An Historical Encyclopedia.* Brooklyn, N.Y.: Carlson Publishing, 1993.

Hinze, Virginia Neal. "Norris Wright Cuney." Master's thesis, Rice University, 1965.

Holt, Thomas. *Black over White: Negro Political Leadership in South Carolina during Reconstruction.* Urbana: University of Illinois Press, 1977.

Hunter, Tera W. "Household Workers in the Making: Afro-American Women in Atlanta and the New South, 1861 to 1920." Ph.D. diss., Yale University, 1990.

Kann, Kenneth. "The Knights of Labor and the Southern Black Worker." *Labor History* 18 (Winter 1977): 49–70.

Lewis, David Levering. *W. E. B. Du Bois: Biography of a Race, 1868–1919*. New York: Henry Holt and Co., 1993.

Logan, Rayford, and Michael Winston, eds. *Dictionary of American Negro Biography*. New York: W.W. Norton and Co., 1982.

Mather, Frank Lincoln, ed. *Who's Who of the Colored Race*. Chicago: n.p., 1915.

Moneyhon, Carl H. *Republicanism in Reconstruction Texas*. Austin: University of Texas Press, 1980.

Reese, James V. "The Evolution of an Early Texas Union: The Screwmen's Benevolent Association of Galveston, 1866–1891." *Southwestern Historical Quarterly* 75 (October 1971): 158–85.

Rice, Lawrence D. *The Negro in Texas, 1874–1900*. Baton Rouge: Louisiana University Press, 1971.

Roses, Lorraine Elena, and Ruth Elizabeth Randolph. *Harlem Renaissance and Beyond: Literary Biographies of 100 Black Women Writers, 1900–1945*. Boston: G. K. Hall and Co., 1990.

Rush, Theresa Gunnels, Carol Fairbanks Myers, and Esther Spring Arata. *Black American Writers Past and Present: A Biographical and Bibliographical Dictionary*. 2 vols. Metuchen, N.J.: Scarecrow Press, 1975.

Schockley, Ann Allen, ed. *Afro-American Women Writers, 1746–1933: An Anthology and Critical Guide*. Boston: G. K. Hall and Co., 1988.

Southern, Eileen. *The Music of Black Americans*. New York: W.W. Norton and Co., 1971.

Spencer, Jon Michael. *Blues and Evil*. Knoxville: University of Kentucky Press, 1993.

Woodson, C[arter] G. "The Cuney Family." *Negro History Bulletin* 11 (March 1948): 123–25, 143.

MAUD CUNEY-HARE

NORRIS WRIGHT CUNEY

NORRIS WRIGHT CUNEY

A Tribune of the Black People

BY

HIS DAUGHTER

MAUD CUNEY HARE

WITH AN INTRODUCTION BY

JAMES S. CLARKSON
Formerly Surveyor of Customs of the Port of New York

THE CRISIS PUBLISHING COMPANY
26 Vesey Street, New York City
1913

ROBERT N. WOOD,
PRINTER,
202 East Ninety-ninth Street, New York

INTRODUCTION

MR. CUNEY'S life, as it is here so faithfully portrayed by his devoted daughter, deserves to be told as much for the inspiration of the many other gallant and intrepid souls in the future who will have to achieve success against many difficulties and discouragements as he did, as in just and deserved honor and tribute to him for the good that he so nobly won to himself and the greater good he so constantly sought and found for his fellow men. His work was always more for humanity than for himself. His kindly nature, his boundless heart, his desire always to be of service to the weak, his sense of justice and spirit of sacrifice, his loyalty to friendship and his high ideals as to every man's duty to his fellow men impressed everyone who ever knew him, and impressed most deeply those who knew him best and therefore knew something of the full quality and measure of his constant and generous service to mankind. Those who knew him from his childhood say that in his younger days, his heart was a shelter for the weak and needy of any and every race; and all who ever came to know him at all, knew that this spirit constantly increased with his years.

I knew him from 1876, when I became acquainted with him at the Republican National Convention at Cincinnati—the Convention in which occurred the famous contest between Blaine and Conkling, a rivalry which divided the party into factions for nearly the whole generation that followed. It was in the storms and contests of that noted Convention, and in those of the compaign preceding for the election of delegates, that were formed the closest and most precious friendships of my political life, and indeed of my whole life. For I, now on reaching the year of grace allotted to man by the Bible have the one testimony to give that the so-called world of politics, instead of being all self-seeking and selfishness, is the one field of human action where more true and generous men are found, and wherein more true and lasting friendships are formed, and more willing and actual sacrifices made, than in any other field of rivalry and competition among men. There are, indeed, many selfish and grasping spirits to be found in that world. But there are in it far more men who are good and generous and patriotic, who form the life guard and decide the destiny of the Nation, and who, from the beginning of the great effort to estab-

lish human freedom on this Continent until
the present day, have been both the inspiring
and sustaining power that has guaranteed and
continued its success.

It was in that Convention at Cincinnati
that I came to know Mr. Fessenden of Con-
necticut, Mr. Hobart of New Jersey, Col. Goodloe
of Kentucky, General Dudley and Mr. Michener
of Indiana, Col. Foraker and Col. Conger .of
Ohio, Senator Elkins of West Virginia, Senator
Platt and Mr. Fassett of New York, Senator
Quay of Pennsylvania, Senator Spooner, Henry
C. Payne and Senator Sawyer of Wisconsin,
Governor Alger of Michigan, Mr. Kerens, Mr.
Van Horn and Mr. Filley of Missouri, Cyrus
Leland of Kansas, Senator Thurston and
Church Howe of Nebraska, Mr. De Young and
Judge Estee of California, and in the South
General Clayton of Arkansas, Governor War-
mouth and Lieut. Gov. Pinchback of Louisi-
ana, Mr. Parsons of Alabama, Mr. Brownlow
of Tennessee and Mr. Cuney of Texas. These
men and scores of others who ought to be mentioned in any roll call of the faithful and useful
men of the Republican Party in those days,
represented the Blaine and Conkling and all
other elements in the party. All these leaders
and all others as well, quickly came to know
Mr. Cuney both in the campaigns for the nomination of the Presidential candidates and in the

campaign for their election afterwards, and to
recognize the sterling and noble qualities of his
manhood and his personality, as well as his
rare and useful abilities as a political leader.
Throughout all the years that followed he kept
a good name and an unshaken influence in the
higher and more controlling councils of the
Party.

In the close friendships that were formed with
ten or twelve of the leaders, all of whom served
together at different times as members of the
National Committee, from twelve to fifteen or
twenty years, Mr. Cuney was always highly
regarded and highly prized by them all. Always
trusted and never doubted by this fellowship
consisting of Fessenden, Hobart, Goodloe, Clarkson, Foraker, Conger, Fassett, Payne, Thurston,
Manley, Dudley, Leland, De Young, Clayton,
and Cuney and at different times five or
six others, Mr. Cuney was always accepted as
one of the most dependable allies and most reliable councillors, and was always insisted upon
as one of those who were to attend all the
inside Party councils and all the important public and private conferences of the National Committee, both during the Presidential Campaigns
and in the intervening years. All these gentlemen as well as the other leading members of the
Committee early came to know the value of his
service and the Party recognized his honest

standards and ideals, and gaining personal liking for him as well, all came to have implicit
faith in him. In the Party Councils at Washington, too, he would often be taken into
private conferences between the President and
other high public and Party officials and was
always one whose judgment was consulted and
whose influence was recognized. He was always
accepted and valued as an intimate friend by
Mr. Blaine through all the years of that great
leader's prominence and popularity. I participated in several interviews of Mr. Cuney with
President Harrison and with various members
of the cabinet, and he impressed them all by
his personal bearing as he had previously done
by his general value and fidelity to the Party.

President Harrison rendered conspicuous
recognition and tribute to him, his ability and
his personal worth and his party rank, by ap-
pointing him collector of the Port of Galveston,
the federal office of first importance in Texas
and scarcely second to the collectorship at New
Orleans in the whole South. His high standing
at home—the best test of any man's worth—
was shown by the fact that nearly all the leading Democratic business men of Galveston and
practically of the whole State, united in a petition to President Harrison endorsing him above
all other Republicans in the State for this office.
His administration of the office fully justified

the President's high estimate of his worth and ability. The records of the Treasury Department still stand as proof that the office under his direction was managed with equal ability and fidelity, and gained the endorsement of the department as being one of the best managed offices in the country. For all time, the superior record he made in that responsible position will stand to his credit and that of his race as being capable of furnishing sufficient ability and devotion for the highest public service.

The traits that I admired most in Mr. Cuney, in addition to those which I have already named, were his pervading and dominating personality, which every one could see and feel as soon as he came to know him, and as being among those who had taught themselves not to grasp but to give, and always to give more than his share; and furthermore and especially his pride in his own race. In this latter respect he showed more intelligence and more courageous loyalty than any man of his own race I have ever known, except Frederick Douglass, the greatest of his people and one of the greatest of Americans, whom I was also privileged to know intimately and with whose unquestioning friendship and good will I was also honored. They both realized, as do all intelligent men of open and fair minds, that the God of Christian people was never capable of being cruel enough to create one race

of human beings to be inferior to all others,
or to be enslaved, oppressed and degraded by
another race, just as they knew that no other
race of the present or the past, could have
endured so many centuries of degradation and
slavery to emerge from it with more of remaining or unextinguished intelligence nor perhaps
with as much of patience and with as little
bitterness of spirit as this darkest of all races
has done. And just as Mr. Cuney's nature was
loyal to his own people, so was it loyal to every
cause and every person he espoused or to which
or whom he was in the least indebted. As
much as any man I have ever known, he was
true to every cause, every duty, and every friend
as any one among them all. To my personal,
actual knowledge, he could have amassed a fortune from the large sums of money, actually
proffered him and urged upon him in several
of the Presidential campaigns from 1876 to 1896
as a reward for his influence and his control
over the Texas delegates to the Republican
National Convention during those years. Mr.
Mark Hanna, who by artificial means changed
the result of the National Convention in 1896,
from what it had been ordered to be by the
instructions electing the delegates in the States
and the Districts of the Nation, gave his unwilling but all important tribute to Mr. Cuney's
loyalty and honesty by naming him to me at

a dinner table in the home of Vice-President Hobart in Washington in 1897 as having been one of the few southern party leaders who could not be swerved by any inducement whatever, to leave the friends with whom he had entered the contest or to desert the candidate for whom he and the delegates he represented had originally declared their preference. This knowledge of the manner in which their father evaded opportunities and temptations so great that not more than one man in the average thousand would have resisted them all, is of more value and a greater source of pride to the faithful daughter who has written this little book now to perpetuate the memory of her father as one of the most useful and devoted men of his race, and to the equally faithful and devoted son whose life is also being lived and fashioned in honor to his father and his principles than if he had left them rich and independent in the treasures of this world.

To me the long years of work and service of Mr. Cuney from the time he became prominent, first in Texas politics in the early 70's, and next and very rapidly in National politics, and his prominent participation in politics until the time of his death in 1898, the important and actual service he rendered his race in all those years; and the example he gave his people in character, influence, and work, formed an era

and example in American history that should
be especially prized and guarded by the Negroes
of America, and by all the darker races throughout the world. Therefore I hope that the
Negro Society for Historical Research which
is being organized by Mr. John E. Bruce and
other capable men in New York City to gather
together all the material still accessible for making a more faithful and complete history of
all that has ever been accomplished in all fields
of endeavor by Negroes in America, is to be provided, as well as all other societies of a similar
character, with a great deal of Mr. Cuney's
correspondence, speeches, and other records of
his work, in those important years. He was
always so modest and reserved that his work
was mainly done out of sight and largely without public record; and it is due to the race
and to the general public, as much as to him,
that his work now be made as fully known as
possible and preserved in prominent and conspicuous form for the future. I shall gladly
do what I can to aid in this. For although
his great work and loyal service were of such
large value to his country and his race during
his life, the example of his life and the true
story of his works alike for his own people
and for all people, told as his daughter has so
lovingly and yet so carefully told it in this
book, will render still more service to mankind

by inspiring and strengthening many other intrepid souls who are to rise from among the many millions of the weak and lowly in the future.

It is difficult for one who knew Mr. Cuney's noble and lovable personal qualities and his rare and loyal political abilities, as intimately as I did, bringing me finally to have for him the friendship and the affection that generally are given alone to kinsmen, to bring this statement to a close, or to keep it within the temperature of a formal public utterance. To me, with an ancestry running back into the days of the Clarksons in England when all of them were Abolitionists, all men and all races have always been alike; all children of the same God, and every man of whatever race or color depending solely on his own merits for affection or esteem. So with all the close friends and fellow members I had in the Republican National Committee for nearly twenty years. In common with all the more prominent and active members of the Committee, I came to have as much faith in and as warm a regard for Mr. Cuney, and Perry H. Carson—another fearless man and loyal soul—as for any of our fellow workers; and I am sure that all of them would give their hearty approval to all I have said of Mr. Cuney in this article both as to his work and his worth. No man was ever more devoted to a party or a cause than he was to the Republican Party.

Indeed, it was dearer to him than his own life—
a life which he so often and so willingly risked
in its support and defense. Even after it had
in its Convention in 1896 so unjustly unseated
him and the other legally elected delegates from
Texas, and placed in their seats men never
elected to the places, and after it had abandoned
its life-long position of placing human rights
above all property rights and all other rights,
and delivered itself over in a sordid surrender
to the control of the dominating material interests of the nation, his deep affection for it still
remained. In the last talk I ever had with him,
he said he regretted its abandonment of the
supreme sentiment of human rights and its
alliance with the sordid interests of the land,
as much for its own sake as for the sake of
his own people thus abandoned by the party of
Abraham Lincoln. He said that while, with its
historic devotion to the rights of all men as
a sentiment that appealed to all good hearts
and to all men of conscience, it had been invincible, it would quickly find that now that it
had put its dependence on money and the money
power, it had lost the faith and the favor of
the people and, sooner or later and at no
distant date, go the way of the Whig Party,
and for the same reasons.

If Mr. Cuney had lived to see his own pro-
phecy so grimly and so terribly fulfilled in the

sensational and epoch-making political year of 1912, no one would have mourned over it, and the national necessity for it, more than he. If he were living now, I am confident he would agree with me and with millions of others who used to take as much pride almost in being Republicans as in being Americans, that the only way left for the once splendid but now repudiated party ever to return to public confidence and respect and to rule in the nation again, is to find its own conscience and return to the principles of Lincoln and the rule of the people; and go back to the ever-supreme duty of creating equal rights and equal chance in life for all men, and especially to the full and final redemption of Lincoln's pledge to the Americans of the colored race, in both their political and their civil rights. The time is now ripe for justice being done as fully to the black race as to the white race. For now many of the better people of the ever implacable and unreasonable South are becoming willing to adjust this wrong, and to eliminate color as a test for the suffrage, and to guard hereafter the purity and the intelligence of the ballot by some sufficient and yet reasonable test as to the qualifications of the voter, by applying it to all men and all races alike. Meantime it is for the Negroes, North as well as South, to have and to show more pride in race and more unity and concert in action, to realize that they have now in their own numbers the power to protect themselves as citizens, to recognize that they as a people have more than paid their debt to the Republican Party, to support hereafter that party which most recognizes the brotherhood of all men, to make themselves if need be the united and acting balance of power in every Presidential and Congressional Election, thus insuring and hastening the day when the black man's rights and protection as a voter and as a husband and a father shall be as secure as the white man's—a day which is sure to come as the next few years shall pass, or the nation as a nation in the end meet the fate that the Republican Party last year met as a party.

I believe that under the blessing of God on the faithful and useful life that Wright Cuney lived, this modest little book by a loyal and worthy daughter, herself such an ornament and such an inspiration to her race, will greatly help in continuing his influence among his people and among all people who would be just, and that it will help in hastening the day when this great Republic shall no longer find itself capable of denying to any man or any woman any of the rights of citizenship or of humanity.

JAMES S. CLARKSON

Tarrytown, N. Y.

February 22, 1913.

CONTENTS

NORRIS WRIGHT CUNEY

CHAPTER I.

EARLY DAYS, 1846–1861.

NORRIS WRIGHT CUNEY was of Negro, Indian and Swiss descent. The Negro and Indian blood came through his mother, Adeline Stuart, for whom free papers were executed by Col. Cuney, and who was born in the State of Virginia. Her mother, Hester Neale Stuart, was of Potomac Indian, Caucasian and Negro blood, and belonged as a slave to a family named Neale of Centreville and Alexandria, Virginia. Our grandmother was a woman of medium height and slender; of olive complexion and regular features, with straight black hair and dark eyes.

The Caucasian blood of my father came principally from the Swiss family of Cuneys who were among the early settlers of Virginia,

coming there with the Archinard family from
Switzerland. About the time of the Louisiana
purchase, they migrated to the new provinces
and became planters in Rapides Parish. Dr.
Samuel Cuney married Edith Wells, whose
children were Stephen, Cæsar, Ben, Samuel,
Richmond and Philip. Philip's first wife was
Charlotte Scott, also of the Wells family. Two
members of the family, the granddaughters of
Edith Wells and Dr. Cuney, Jane and Florida,
over 80 years of age in 1912, still lived on the
old plantation at Sugar Bend, Louisiana.

When the political designations originated
in 1824, my white grandfather, Col. Philip N.
Cuney, who was an ardent politician, followed
the Whig division of the Southern Democracy.
These were days of intense party feeling, and
for years a feud existed between the two political
parties in the Parish of Rapides on Red River,
Louisiana. In 1827, on a sandbar opposite
Natchez, a duel was fought, the principals being
Dr. Maddox, Major Wright and the Blanchards
on one side, the Wells, the Bowies and the
Cuneys on the other. All the parties engaged
were men of wealth and standing. The Wells
and Maddox families remained in the Parish,
while the Bowies and Cuneys joined those
Americans who migrated to Texas, the Bowies
going in 1827 and the Cuneys in 1842. One of
the participants in the Red River fight, James

Bowie, of "Bowie knife" fame, became a devoted patriot of the State of Texas and one of the martyrs of the Alamo.

When Col. Philip Cuney came to Texas with his family, he settled in Waller County, near Hempstead, on the east side of the Brazos River. Here, in the heart of the cotton and melon belt, he maintained a large plantation and held slaves, among whom was my grandmother, mentioned above, Adeline Stuart, who bore him eight children and whom he eventually set free. There were extensive areas of cotton under cultivation, while for miles stretched prairies full of grazing herds of buffalo, and woods through which roamed wandering Indian tribes. At that time the Brazos River, stocked with fish and alligator, was not open to trade, a wide contrast to the busy stream of to-day with its many steamer ports and thriving harbor at Velasco.

Here the Cuney clan became part of that great drama by which Texas was made a slave empire and annexed to the United States by the Mexican War.

In the midst of that war, on May 12, 1846, my father was born at "Sunnyside," the plantation on the Brazos River owned by his father, Col. Philip Cuney. He was the fourth of eight children, all of whom, except two, were born at "Sunnyside." All of the children resembled the mother, except one of the two daughters who was a blonde like her father. Joseph, the second son, had his father's blue eyes and the mother's jet-black hair. My father was the darkest of the children, with his mother's olive complexion, brown eyes and black hair. In 1853, when father was seven years of age, the family moved to Houston and the two older boys were sent to Pittsburgh to attend school.

My grandmother was an especially active and industrious little woman who kept everyone about her busy whenever she could find anything for them to do. The boys were always at work around the home, but my father was said to be the most difficult of the children, and always shirked home work. He never became a "handy-man around the house." What he delighted in was playing the bass-violin as taught him by "Henry the fiddler." Music of any kind was a rare thing in Houston in those days. The town was the center for country-trade and the little boy "Wright," playing his large instrument, was often called upon to furnish pleasure to admiring crowds.

In 1859, when father was 13 years of age, he was sent to Pittsburgh, Pa., to join his brothers, Nelson and Joseph, at school. The boys attended the Wyle Street School, a colored institution taught by George B. Vashon.

There was a ring of bad boys at the school

and they came and went as they pleased. Whenever the principal attempted to correct them, they would run and get their hats, and hastening through the back door, would cry out mockingly, "Good-day, Mr. Vashon." One day a boy named David Coffee, with the assistance of others threw Mr. Vashon on the floor, held him down, and pulled his long black whiskers. Mr. Vashon, proud of his whiskers, could not have suffered a greater indignity. My father was much younger than any of these boys. He looked on full of wrath while the boys were teasing Mr. Vashon, until he could stand it no longer. The other children were amazed, but did not know what to do. Finally father went at the mischievous ones single-handed, with so much vim and anger, that they ran from the room. So greatly surprised were they at my father's temerity in attacking them, they did not stay to fight him.

He had many friends among the schoolchildren; in fact he and his brothers were very much liked by all of their playmates, good and bad. They seemed to their comrades very different, with their shy Texas manners and ways, exciting great curiosity, but they were really liked because of their frank friendliness. All of the brothers took their studies seriously and stood well up in their classes.

Their leisure was spent in fishing, rowing

and sailing in and about the beautiful pebble-
bottomed Allegheny River, and often in later
years they would tell us of those days of
pleasure.

It was intended that the boys should attend
Oberlin College, but as the war came on in 1861,
they were cut off from the allowance of money
from home.

CHAPTER II.

THE YOUTH, 1861–1868.

WHEN on April 15, 1861, President Lincoln issued a call for volunteers, my Uncle, Joseph Cuney, who had just reached manhood, left Pittsburgh with the 63rd Pennsylvania Volunteers, while father remained at school in Pittsburgh.

During the war my Uncle Joe had passed a number of times through the little town of Centreville in Fairfax County, Virginia. At that time he had no idea of its personal interest and importance to him. Later his mother wrote him to go to her birthplace, Centreville, and find her mother, Hester Neale Stuart. Centreville had been so over-run by both Confederate and Union armies during the war, that many people had left the place. Hester Stuart had settled in Alexandria, Virginia, where she was subsequently found living with relatives. My grandmother, who had not seen her mother for forty years, was deeply rejoiced to find her. My great-grandmother finally died at the age of one hundred.

Uncle Joe had expected my father to stay
at Pittsburgh, but the excitement became too
great for him to content himself with studies.
In 1863, at the age of 17, he went to St.
Louis, thence to Cincinnati, spending many
months on the boats of the Mississippi River.

While steamboating on the old Grey Eagle
he was often at New Orleans. There he met
and formed life friendships with young men
who, as Col. James Lewis and Lieut. Gov. Pinchback, later became prominent in the Reconstruction period in the State of Louisiana.

At the close of the war father returned to
Texas and settled at Galveston, the sister city
of his old home, Houston. He was eager to
acquire knowledge and as his education had
been interrupted by the unsettled conditions
and misfortune of war, he now began a period
of self-education, studying the best literature
and reading law.

It was not strange that Galveston with her
oleander-bordered streets and "much sounding
sea" should have attracted him as a home city.
Galveston was the garden spot of Texas. For
thirty miles the Gulf of Mexico washed the
island. The deep white sand girded about by the
waves was packed hard and firm. Breezes
fresh from the Gulf mingled with odors of
oleander, roses, and cape jasmine from the city
gardens. The great surf broke upon the beach,

fringing the shore with foam. The breakers of deep blue, growing in strength as they neared the shore—high, one above the other, the murmur increasing into a roar, lashed and laved the glistening sands with that endless and fascinating sound of the sea for which an exiled native ever yearns.

To-day one must drive far out from the city to see the beach as father saw it forty years ago, for the wooing of Galveston by the sea has been balked by the great sea wall.

The city, terribly stricken twelve years ago by the flood, counted the loss of thousands of lives and untold damage to property. My father's mother, a dear little old lady of 86 years, was ill at the time, and she with other relatives was among the lost. The sea, "where the Infinite hath dwelling," is the last resting place of the household of Nelson Cuney—wife, son and mother.

In 1867, shortly after father settled in Galveston, a yellow fever epidemic of a most virulent form broke out in the city and the neighboring towns. In Galveston, eighteen hundred persons died. It was difficult to find nurses to care for the sick because of the fear of contagion.

Father, always sensitive to suffering in others, tender-hearted and ever willing to sacrifice himself, volunteered as nurse. For months he nursed yellow fever patients, both white and black, in Galveston, Brenham, Houston, Navasota and Hempstead. He finally contracted the disease himself, but rapidly recovered.

At this time Uncle Joseph returned to Texas and, with the exception of the daughter Jennie who was sent to Mannheim in Baden, Germany, with Miss Josephine Barbour, the fiancée of Joseph, to attend Madame Nichol's Institute for Young Ladies, grandmother with the remainder of the family now made Galveston their home.

CHAPTER III.

ENTRANCE INTO POLITICS, 1869–1872.

FATHER was twenty-one years of age when he first heard of those words which James G. Blaine uttered in the House of Representatives: —"There is no protection you can extend to a man so effective and conclusive as the power to protect himself. And in assuring protection to the loyal citizens you assure permanency to the government. The bestowal of suffrage is therefore not merely the discharge of a personal obligation toward those who are enfranchised; but it is the most far-sighted provision against social disorder, the surest guarantee of peace, prosperity and public justice." From this time on he became one of Mr. Blaine's warmest admirers.

Texas having rejected the 14th amendment with other southern states, was at this time without representation in Congress, and military government was established. Texas and Louisiana, comprising the Fifth District, were under the command of Gen. Sheridan.

In 1860, when Texas was drawn into seces-

sion, out of a total assessed property valuation
of $225,000,000, slaves comprised $85,000,000,
there being 140,000 held in the State. Texas
now faced the problem of converting this mass
of human property into intelligent American
citizens. Many Texans refused to accept the
fact that the Negro was "free and equal" and
stopped at nothing to prevent him from enjoying civic and political rights.

The Ku Klux Klan and the Democrats opposed every policy of reconstruction and were
determined by force and intimidation to keep
the Negro from the polls. In the State election
of 1869, which was the twelfth since Texas
ceased to be a Republic, Edmund J. Davis, Republican, received a plurality of 809 votes over
Andrew J. Hamilton. Mr. Davis stood for
justice to all men and allowed neither intimidation nor bribery to change his course. The
majority of the whites meant at all costs to
suppress the Negro vote. Gov. Davis was derided by the opposition, who declared that he
was the candidate of the military, carpet-bag-
gers and Negroes. He enjoyed, however, the
support of many of the good men of the State
irrespective of party affiliation. At the close
of the year 1870, Texas was restored to the
Union.

Father, young, intensely patriotic, eager for
service and possessing unlimited faith in the

Negro race, entered into public service during this troublesome period. He was appointed Sergeant-at-Arms of the Twelfth Texas Legislature. While occupying this position, he became warmly attached to the Republican Governor, Edmund J. Davis, and thereafter followed the fortunes of the Republican Party in Texas.

After the declaration of freedom the first thought for the man of color was not only to provide him with means of livelihood, but to educate him for intelligent and patriotic citizenship. The work of the Freedman's Bureau was ably assisted by Mission Schools founded by Northern philanthropy. Church organizations—the Baptist, the Methodist Episcopal and the Congregational, rapidly established schools throughout the State. The Congregationalists from the first set their face against the isolation of the colored race by race distinction and gave largely through the American Missionary Association. Both teachers and funds were sent to further education in the State. Wiley University, one of our first and best educational institutions, was founded in 1873 by the Freedman's Aid and Southern Education Society of the Methodist Episcopal Church.

As early as 1845, ineffectual effort had been made to establish free public schools in Texas. In 1866, renewed effort was made through

regulations framed by the constitution, and in
1869, provision was made to add to the public
school fund the proceeds of the sale of all
the public lands of the commonwealth—a provision declared to be "entirely unequalled in
magnitude and unsurpassed in nobility of spirit
in the history of the other States of the Union."

By the constitution of 1869, the legislature
was authorized to divide the State into school
districts, each of which was to be subject to
the supervision of a board of school directors
with full control over all the schools, school-
houses and school funds within their jurisdiction.

My father became early interested in educational matters and believed that the Negro
should receive his public education from the
general school funds and not from that derived
from the Negro tax-payers alone. On July 17,
1871, he was appointed one of the School
Directors for Galveston County, and was untiring in his efforts to advance popular education
in the State.

About this time, father met and fell in love
with Adelina Dowdie, and was married on July
5, 1871. Mother was the youngest of six sisters,
known as "the handsome Dowdie girls," and was
the daughter of a white planter of Woodville,
Miss., who had migrated to Texas in 1864. Her
mother was a mulatto slave. At the time of her

marriage my mother was a girl of only sixteen, and was preparing for the profession of teaching. She was small in figure, of fair complexion, with large grey eyes and curly black hair. She was of a most unselfish disposition, working incessantly for the poor, active in charitable organizations and always in the lead in matters of social uplift. She was religious without being pious. Always bubbling over with fun, her Christianity was one of sunshine and cheerfulness. Possessing a beautiful, dramatic soprano voice, she sang publicly whenever her services could benefit some good cause. Having decided on public school teaching as her life work, she was naturally interested in educational matters and was a true helpmeet to father in his work to better school conditions in the State.

CHAPTER IV.

Early Leadership, 1872–1875.

THE campaign of 1872 was a most interesting one, in that, for the first time in the history of the Union, the freedman voted for presidential electors. The Republicans met in Philadelphia and nominated President Grant for a second term. For the first time, father was elected a delegate to a National Convention. Among the new issues advanced by the platform, the old one, vital to the Negro, held its place. It was declared that "complete liberty and exact equality in the enjoyment of all civil, political and public rights should be established and effectually maintained throughout the Union by appropriate Federal and State Legislation."

Father had now been in Government employ for some months. February 1, 1872, he was appointed Inspector of Customs for the District of Texas. Nathan Patten, who was appointed Collector of Customs, in the Fall of 1869, was a splendid man and a good friend.

From now on, my father's life was dedicated to the upbuilding of his race. After studying

Mrs. N. Wright Cuney

the situation, he became convinced that in the ballot lay the Negro's chance for self-protection and he never once ceased to fight for this end. He worked always for the franchise for all men worthy of the name of citizen. He favored all institutions that taught an appreciation of State and civic duties and held true manhood the ideal for all races of men.

In the early development of the Negro in the South, the secret societies were among the most helpful forces. The first Masonic Lodge was established in Texas in 1833, before the days of the Republic. In 1873, the Negro Masons of Texas organized a Grand Lodge with four subordinate Lodges located at Galveston, Houston, Austin and San Antonio. The Masonic Order based on principles of "Liberality, Brotherly Love and Charity" appealed to father. He early joined the organization and on June 24, 1874, he was duly elected and appointed R. W. Deputy Grand-master of the M. W. K. S. G. Lodge for the State of Kansas and jurisdiction on the continent of North America.

The year 1875 marked the 100th since Masonry was revealed to the colored men of this country, and the Prince Hall Lodge held appropriate demonstrations in Boston, Mass., June 25, 1875. Father, as P. M. Mason and R. W. Deputy Grand-master for the State of Kansas and jurisdiction, was commissioned to assist in the proceedings in Boston. There they protested against those who continued to refuse to acknowledge or recognize members of the Negro race as Masons, and met also to "do all within our power to remove the hateful spirit of caste— to the end that equity of justice shall become the supreme and governing principle of the American people—to make smooth the ways of children and by education to lead them in those paths of knowledge in which shall be found true happiness in this world and in that to come."

From April 28, 1870 to January 14, 1874, Edmund J. Davis was, by election, again the Governor of the State of Texas. There were two factions among the Republicans; the Unionists, who supported A. J. Hamilton, and the Regulars. When, in 1873, Mr. Davis ran for re-election, he received but little support from the Union Republicans and Richard Coke, the Democratic candidate, was elected. Mr. Davis had been unflinching in prosecuting measures necessary to protect the enfranchised Negro, and while greatly criticised by his opponents because of his affiliation with the colored men of the State, the historians admit that he was a sincere public servant, of good character, personal honesty and a worthy citizen. Though defeated in the State election, the Davis faction continued to control the party machinery in Texas.

In the state convention the Republicans had emphasized the necessity of maintaining a system of free schools with improvements as experience had shown to be desirable. Father was appointed, at this time, the Secretary of the Republican State Executive Committee.

Always having the courage to fight for what he believed right, father never submitted peacefully to an injustice. Early in January, having an altercation with Deputy Marshal Dewees over a bill of costs, the daily press severely criticised him for "insulting and assaulting the United States Marshal."

In an open letter appearing in the Galveston "News," January 12, 1875, father wrote:—"I had hoped not to have to say anything in public about the unpleasant matter; but things have taken such a course as to make it imperative that I do so. I claim to have some knowledge of the civility that should subsist between gentlemen, and I always endeavor to govern myself accordingly. I did not insult Mr. Dewees. He insulted and assaulted me and I exercised the God-given right of self-defense and resented his insult. I believe it is generally agreed among lawyers that when a party is presented with a bill of costs that he may request the party presenting it, to itemize it, and it is the latter's duty to do so. This is all I did and I did it in a respectful and gentlemanly manner.

"As to the apology, I will state that Mr. Dewees sent for me, asked me into his private office and told me to be seated; after which he said to me that he had sent for me to see if we could not settle our difficulty without any more fighting. I told him he had been doing the fighting; that I was acting in self-defense. He said he had done me an injustice and felt that he owed me an apology; that he was a man of quick temper and had acted indiscreetly. I accepted his apology and told him that I myself had a bad temper, but always tried to subordinate it to what was becoming a gentleman.

"I told him there was no wounded honor on my part, that it was simply tit for tat between him and me; that it was true I got little the worse of it and the only reason I did not hurt him was because I could get nothing to hurt him with. He smiled and said yes, it was true he had little the best of it because he was where he could get material to fight with. He then presented me the itemized bill, whereupon I paid it. I arose to go and he assured me that if we ever had any business together in the future, that I should find him a straightforward and upright man. There was a third party present the time this transpired. If I am the aggressor in this matter and have gone into the United States Marshal's office and assaulted the chief officer in charge, and there were witnesses present as stated in the said article, why am I not arrested and made to pay the penalty for violating the public peace? No one regrets more than I do that this affair occurred, but having occurred, I feel conscious that I have acted honorably throughout the whole affair."

In the State campaign of this Spring, father, then a young man of 29 years, attracted the notice of both parties. The white Radicals of the Hempstead Convention, disgruntled at the holding of a caucus by colored men, declared "it would be a good thing for the Republican Party, if the Negroes would split and half of them would join the Democratic Party." "Never again," they added, "will we participate in a Radical Convention where Negroes lead. Think of it—there is Cuney, living in the most advanced and wealthiest community of the State (Galveston), published to his fellow-citizens as holding high place in our party organization."

An incident which took place in Galveston that Fall proved how little disturbed were the "wealthiest and most advanced" citizens because a man of Negro blood living among them was recognized in the councils of the Republican Party. Galveston was a growing sea-port town, ambitious to develop a harbor second to none on the Gulf of Mexico. Aware of the possibilities and interested in her shipping industry, bankers, importers and wholesale merchants agreed to meet at the Cotton Exchange on the 20th day of October, 1875 for consultation "with a view to devise and inaugurate, in co-operation with the municipal authorities, measures to secure dikes or levees around the city." Father was among those citizens requested to meet at the Cotton Exchange.

Though a young man, he was rapidly gaining the confidence and esteem of the thoughtful men of the community. Believing that he would make an efficient public servant, the Republicans nominated him for Mayor of Galveston. R. L. Fulton was the Democratic candidate and won the election. In later years, Mr. Fulton stated;—"In the city election of 1875, I had the satisfaction of defeating Mr. Cuney for the position of Mayor and at the same time of learning of some of his excellent qualities as a public man. He has exercised a remarkable influence on the politics of this city, and invariably in the interest of sound policy and honest government."

CHAPTER V.

POLITICAL CAREER, 1876–1880.

EARLY in the year 1876, the Senatorial District comprising the counties of Galveston, Brazoria and Matagorda, held a convention to nominate members of the Legislature. For Senator, A. P. McCormick received a majority and his nomination was made unanimous, while the name of N. W. Cuney was received with acclamation as the nominee for "Floater," as was called the Representative of that part of the people over and above the apportionment. In the election father met with defeat.

The new Legislature assembled on the 18th of April. The conditions in the State were still unsettled—many evils were complained of, and in order that they might be more easily corrected, a new constitution was drafted. Governor Coke was re-elected and found it necessary in some instances to appeal to military force. Labor troubles broke out in Galveston, and a strike owing to a dispute over the question of wages was launched. It soon assumed ugly proportions. One of the leaders of the strike,

Michael Burns, presiding at a general mass
meeting called at the Court House, declared that
if matters were not settled satisfactorily to the
strikers, they would destroy trains and locomo-
tives and thus cause the company greater
loss than the increase of wages asked for. My
father sprang to his feet and answered the
speaker. An onlooker wrote: "At the meeting
last evening, Mr. Wright Cuney, a colored man
and one of the most intelligent of his race in
the State, gave the men good advice. Mr. Cuney
knows but too well that the poor, deluded colored
men who are now on a strike in this city, are
but the tools of some designing white men who
have aspirations—political and otherwise, and
he did not hesitate to tell them so. Mr. Cuney's
address was eminently sensible and to the
point." It was true that the grievances of the
strikers were not important enough to demand
public sympathy or to cause suffering of the
families depending upon them. The lawless
element made it an excuse for street riots; acts
of violence were committed and it became necessary for Mayor Stone to issue a proclamation
threatening to call on the militia to preserve
public order. Rioting was general. Father
mingling with the crowds on the street, was
called for and stood amid hoots of the rabid
faction, to address the mob. He reminded the
crowd that the muttered threats of violence

which he had heard were something that he
deeply regretted. He said to the colored men
that for the past forty-eight hours they had been
parading the streets of the city, creating all
sorts of discord and stirring up bad blood,
which had culminated in the shooting affair on
Market Street. The most respectable number
the strikers had ever been able to muster did
not equal three hunded men, and as there were
1500 laborers, he asked what that handful of
malcontents hoped to accomplish by their turbulent demonstrations, except riot and bloodshed, and the destruction of their own best interests. He asked the strikers what they could
do in the prosecution of their disorders, and told
them that there were over seven hundred armed
men—trained soldiers in the city, who could an-
nihilate them all in an hour; and if they could
not, he said, that in the city of Houston there
were 1,000 men under arms who could be
brought to this city within two hours to accomplish that bloody work. He deprecated in
the severest terms the follies into which the
colored men had fallen, and said that they were
not supported by the white men nor by the full
strength of their own color. He said that every
good citizen would be found on the side of the
law when the strike was carried to the extent
where collisions would result, and that the
strikers would in the end be the sufferers for

the foolishness of which they had already been guilty, in a vain attempt to revolutionize the industrial interests of the city. He told the colored men to disperse and go to their homes, and on the morrow to go out and try to get work to do at some price so they might protect their wives and children from want.

In conclusion, he read Mayor Stone's proclamation, and it was reported that "he, in an eloquent and forcible manner appealed to his race to heed his warning and go peacefully to their homes and stay there. He never for a moment lost control of his temper or yielded the fact that the law must be maintained." The strike was finally settled with satisfaction to the men and their employers.

Scarcely had the labor situation cleared before there was race discrimination to contend with.— Greenwall as theatrical manager had refused a colored woman, Mary Miller, a desired seat in the theatre. The colored citizens on March 3 held an indignation meeting denouncing Hon. Amos Morrill, U. S. District Judge, in the case of Greenwall. Greenwall had been indicted, tried, convicted, and fined $500 for violation of the Civil Rights Act. Having no property subject to execution and sale, he was dismissed. Judge Morrill was arraigned by the colored people for not ordering Greenwall to remain in the custody of the Sheriff until the fine was paid. The San Antonio (Daily) *Express*, independent, in reporting the proceedings, noted, "The leading speech at the meeting was made by N. W. Cuney, the most talented man of the colored race we know in the State. The only fault of the speech is its extreme rashness of denunciation of the Judge. We know nothing of the case nor have we examined the law, but after that speech, something will have to be done, we imagine."

Father had continued to hold his position as Inspector of Customs, to which he was appointed in 1872. In the matter of patronage, he criticised Collector Shields as being influenced by prejudice. Friction between himself and the Collector resulted in his dismissal. He protested against the action of the Collector and request was made for the cause of his removal and demand made for his re-instatement. Mayor Stone, with a large number of leading citizens formed a petition of 100 names, forwarded the same to the Secretary of the Treasury and in unstinted terms gave their endorsement to his good character and competency.

The "Galveston Daily News" editorial read, "The summary dismissal of Wright Cuney from his position as Inspector in the Customs House at this port, seems to be in conflict with the precedent established under the civil service measures of the present administration at Washington, in the case of Marshall Purnell who was permitted to make his defense on the charges preferred against him, by those who sought to secure his summary removal from office. Cuney is making an effort to have himself re-established in the position from which he was removed, and he is strongly backed by many of the best business men of this city who commend his capacities for the position and vouch for his character as a man. In the recent troubles which have prevailed in this city, Cuney has shown himself to be above the average of his race— a friend of law and public tranquillity, and by the part he bore in restoring order among the turbulent Negroes who had given themselves to riotous measures, he made many friends who have availed themselves of this occasion to say a good word in his behalf."

The result was that Collector Shields was ordered peremptorily to place him on duty. Gov. Coke, commenting on the case remarked, "Cuney is a spry sort of a fellow."

In June the Republican National Convention was held at Cincinnati, Ohio, and Rutherford B. Hayes was nominated for President. Father was sent as a delegate from the Fifth Congressional District of Texas, and thus had the opportunity of becoming acquainted with the statesmen who later became his good friends—

Allison, Blaine, Harrison, Hobart, Fessenden, Platt and the younger man, James S. Clarkson.

The Presidential election of 1876 was bitter. Following the inauguration of Pres. Hayes, the people of the country were more interested in financial and industrial issues than they were in the welfare of the colored people of the South. Military rule had been discontinued but the Southland was far from being at peace.

In Mr. Blaine's speech in the 45th Congress, respecting the conduct of elections in the South, he declared, "The colored citizen is most unhappily situated; his right of suffrage is but a hollow mockery; it holds to his ear the word of promise but breaks it always to his hope, and he ends only in being made the unwilling instrument of increasing the political strength of that party from which he suffered ever-tightening fetters when he was made free. He resembles indeed those unhappy captives in the East who, deprived of their birthright, are compelled to yield their strength to the aggrandizement of the monarch from whose tyrannies they have most to fear, and to fight against the power from which alone deliverance might be expected. The franchise intended for the shield and defense of the Negro has been turned against him and against his friends and has vastly increased the power of those from whom he has nothing to hope and everything to dread."

The Federal Government had proved itself powerless to conquer the unconquered prejudice of the South. The colored man had, in many cases, the suffrage absolutely denied or he was threatened by mobs; frauds were perpetrated— innocent men were murdered for daring to be Republicans. In Texas, a colored voter having declared his intention of deserting the Union Labor Party and supporting the Republicans, was taken from his home by a masked band of men and shot. In New Orleans a Baptist clergy- man was driven from his home and family by an armed mob for an offense no greater than that of helping to organize a Republican meet- ing. There now began a large exodus of the colored population of the South. Conventions of colored men were called to consider the con- dition of the race and to discuss the emigra- tion movement. There was discouragement and discontent everywhere.

President Lincoln had been a firm believer in African colonization. Indeed, in December of 1861, he had recommended a provision for col- onizing the slaves set free by war, but nothing came of the suggestion. Earnest men were thoughtfully weighing the advantages and dis- advantages of colonization.

Father, when asked if he thought the colored

people of the South would be benefited by such
a movement, replied: "No, I cannot see wherein
they would gain anything. They are so thoroughly identified with the perpetuity of our
American institutions, that it seems to me to
be rather late for them now to seek homes in
a new country with the customs, government
and people of which they are thoroughly unac-
quainted. There is much more glory, honor and
gain for the colored man here in the land of his
birth, and here he should stay and fight his
way to the front. As a race, it rests with him
to carve out his own character, which will demand the proper recognition here as soon as
elsewhere."

When asked if he thought the condition of
the colored people in his own section warranted
them in making a change, he answered: "No,
I do not think that the colored people of this
section would be justified in emigrating in a
body. Individually, some of them might per-
chance, improve their condition by going elsewhere, just as other people do, and this they
will continue to do, just as other people. Negroes
are human beings and should be considered
from that standpoint, if people would understand them as a race. In their actions and
manner of life, they are prompted by very
much the same motives actuating others of the
human family."

In the matter of education the outlook was
growing brighter for the colored youth in Texas.
In readjusting relations to the new conditions
succeeding the days of Reconstruction, a more
liberal provision was made for the support of
the public schools. In 1878, by an act of the
State Legislature, the Prairie View State Nor-
mal and Industrial Institute for colored youth
was founded. The location was that of the
old plantation of Col. Kirby, which was on a
beautiful prairie near Hempstead, not many
miles from the birthplace of my father, in
Waller County. What was once the dwelling
house of the master of the plantation is now
the Chemical Laboratory and Lecture Room.
Here since 1885, 1030 students have received
their training for teachers. The growth of the
school has been very rapid. Prof. E. L. Black-
shear, who has held the position for fourteen
years, is the Superintendent. Mr. Wade C.
Rollins is the efficient Secretary and Treasurer.
Mr. Rollins states:

"Your father was interested in this school
and was instrumental in many ways in having
a large number of young colored men attend
it, among them myself. He secured for me a
scholarship here for three successive years, and
whatever of success I may have attained to this
point, is in large measure due to his kindness
and foresight." The Institution is supported

by annual appropriations made by the Commonwealth and by income from tuition fees.

At this time, in the public schools of Galveston, the trustees were willing to employ white teachers for public schools should not enough colored teachers be obtained. An advertisement appearing for applicants for positions in the free schools Dec. 17, 1881, read "white and colored applicants will be examined in different rooms."

The first innovation was in the fall when they held the examinations at different times and places—a step backward from former procedure. Father joined other colored citizens in protesting against so unnecessary an arrangement. The authorities were disposed to treat the colored teachers and pupils fairly, but segregation continues to be practised in the public schools.

As one of the School Directors, father was interested in having school sessions lengthened. By reforms in the school law, under the administration of Gov. Roberts a larger number of children were taught and for a longer school term than ever before. Gov. Roberts had been re-elected in 1880, with Joseph D. Sayers as Lieutenant-Governor. Mr. Sayers, though a Democrat, proved to be a man of broad sympathies and a true, good friend to the colored people.

In June, 1880, father was sent as a delegate to the Republican National Convention which

met in Chicago. The Convention was memorable
in political annals for its large number of able
men and brilliant display of oratory. Benjamin
Harrison of Indiana, C. A. Boutelle of Maine,
George F. Hoar and H. C. Lodge of Massachusetts, Matthew Quay of Pennsylvania, James
S. Clarkson of Iowa and the colored Senator
from Mississippi, Blanche K. Bruce, were some
of the eminent public men in attendance. There
had been an inclination for the renomination
of Gen. Grant, but there was also warm enthusiasm for Blaine. As the 36th ballot opened,
delegations which had been voting for Blaine
and Sherman changed to Garfield, who represented a liberal and progressive Republicanism.
Father voted 35 times for James G. Blaine.
James A. Garfield and Chester A. Arthur received the nominations.

The Collector of Customs for the port of Galveston was now Col. A. G. Malloy. On June 1,
1881, father received his appointment as Chief
Inspector of Customs. Desiring to enter more
fully into the service of the people, he became
a candidate for Alderman in the city campaign
in March and was elected Alderman of the 12th
ward—a ward composed of 1801 persons—1120
white and 681 colored. On the 18th of the month
he was removed from his position as Chief
Inspector of Customs, on account of being elected

and qualifying as an Alderman. The matter occasioned much comment.

The facts were as follows:

Previous to the election, Congressman Thomas Ochiltree had written, stating positively upon the authority of Assistant Secretary of the Treasury J. C. New, that acceptance of the position of Alderman would in no possible manner affect his government position. After receiving the information, father thought no more of the matter until, on boarding the steamship "Whitney" to discharge his duties as Inspector, Mr. Baxter, a Custom House employé, told him that he had been removed from his position and that his services would not be needed. He went at once to General Malloy, the Collector, who denied having issued the order. Later on he threw the responsibility on the Deputy-Collector. Father, speaking in very plain language, charged him with a lack of official courtesy and a desire to insult him by the manner in which he had acted.

A few days later a telegram came from Acting Secretary French of the Treasury Department, stating that in accordance with the Executive order of Ex-President Grant issued in Jan. 1873, Mr. Cuney had vacated his official position as Inspector. Father was not satisfied with the ruling and submitted the matter to President Arthur, who finally disposed of it by declaring Grant's order to be still in force and that the two offices could not be held at the same time; but he was given the right of choosing which one of the offices he would resign. There was without doubt, duplicity on the part of the Custom House officials.

Whatever the merits or demerits of the case, he was asked to choose between the two positions. Having decided to be independent of Government office, father stated he would prefer going into business which would not interfere with his holding the position of Alderman, for he had contested for the latter office with the belief that he could fill the position honorably and be of service to his constituents. Thus he left the Customs Service which he was to re-enter eight years later, as the chief official at Galveston.

Among the comments on his resignation was the following: "It is but fair to add that Mr. Cuney is a colored man of unusual mental culture and enjoys the esteem and confidence of all who know him. He is a Republican from principle and not even the most extreme opponent of civil rights has ever attributed to him any but the purest and most honorable actions in politics and private life."

Father soon had occasion to visit Austin. Upon his return he was interrogated as to his interest in having the Legislature establish a school for deaf, dumb, and blind colored youth.

He replied: "It is all a mistake. I went to
Austin solely on private business. I discussed
the school matter with a few legislators while
there, it is true, but I even refused to sign a
petition to establish such an Asylum. Had
the memorial been drawn to read that the State
should make provision for all her unfortunates,
I certainly should have endorsed it, but I do
not seek special legislation for the Negro. Under
the constitution of our common country he is
taxed the same as other men and the unfortunate
of the race are entitled to the same consideration.
At present the only two public institutions open
to him are the penitentiary and the lunatic asylum. The asylums for the blind, deaf and dumb,
the Agricultural and Mechanical College and the
State University are all closed to him. It is
a sad travesty upon humanity and justice that
the State of Texas accepted gifts of public
lands for the endowment of an Agricultural and
Mechanical College for the benefit of the whole
people, and bars a large proportion of her population because they were born black; that the
tax-collectors make no discriminations, yet when
a man is born deaf and dumb or a man is
stricken with blindness, a black skin is an
insurmountable barrier to that care and attention which should be accorded by right." Questioned as to Social Equality, he replied, "No,
I do not ask for social equality for my race.

That is a matter no law can touch. Men associate with men they find congenial, but in matters of education and State charity there certainly should be no distinction. There is a
clause in our State constitution separating the
schools. This brands the colored race as an
inferior one. I think it would be better to leave
such matters to the local school trustees."

The approach of the State elections of 1882
caused less excitement than usual; it was an off
year politically, no national interests being at
stake. When, in July, the Republican County
Convention assembled, father, who was a member
of the Executive Committee, and his political
rival, Colonel A. G. Malloy, were selected among
others as delegates to the State Convention
which was to meet at Austin. At the Convention, father was elected temporary chairman.
The Convention decided to support at the
approaching election of the State officers, "candidates who come before the people for suffrage
as independents." A committee of which father
was chairman, was named "to confer with other
anti-Bourbon organizations and elements of opposition and reach a conclusion as to whom
among Independent candidates the Republicans
should support." Father entered the campaign
in October as a candidate for the legislature,
for the 66th District, composed of the counties

of Galveston, Brazoria, Matagorda and Wharton, with the following platform:

"*Education.* Our school term is too short. I am an advocate for the extension of our School term to nine months during the year. Our scholastic age must be changed. I favor the extenson of our scholastic age from 7 to 18 years. In order to do this I am in favor of an amendment to the Constitution, levying specific tax for the support of public education. I am in favor of the sale of the Public School Lands to actual settlers only.

"*Jury Laws.* I am in favor of a revision of the Jury Laws, to the end that jurors must be drawn from the body of the people.

"*Public Roads.* I am in favor of the repeal of the present Road Law, and the enactment of another by which the short term convict labor of the State may be used for such purposes, and the confinement to labor within the walls of the penitentiary of all others, in order that they may not be brought in competition with the industry of the people.

"*Houses of Refuge.* I am in favor of the erection by the State of suitable houses of Refuge for juvenile offenders, in order that they may not as now, be consigned to the penitentiary and compelled to associate with hardened criminals.

"I shall visit all the counties of the District,

and will be pleased to divide time with my opponents in discussing before the people these
issues."

One comment read:—"The candidate, N. W.
Cuney, is a man of excellent character and competent ability, large political experience and
varied and careful observation. Few men have
deeper convictions and still fewer have his
capacity for their forcible expression either in
public or private life. His long experience in
the customs has given him ample knowledge of
commerce and general business, while his knowledge of men is exceptionally great."   The
Democratic press noted that "N. W. Cuney, the
Independent candidate for the Legislature from
the 66th District, is a colored man, but we must
confess that his platform is a much better one
than those put forward by white candidates.
One may not like Cuney, but one has to acknowledge that his platform is excellent."

In the election father met with defeat. The
movement for a change of the law relating to
convict labor was one in which father was very
much in earnest. At his suggestion, meetings
were called and resolutions adopted condemning
the practice of hiring out convicts as farm
laborers for small pay, thus prolonging unnec-
essarily their term of punishment, no heed being
taken by the authorities of the wrongs inflicted
upon the law-breakers while working out a

pecuniary fine on the farm. He declared that the convict law of the State in its practical working was a direct violation of the constitution of the United States. It was decided to present a petition to the Legislature praying for a repeal of the law, and father was among the citizens appointed to memorialize the Legislature on the subject.

CHAPTER VI.

In Business.

Desirous of becoming independent of public office, father, early in the year of 1883, entered the business of stevedoring, employing about 500 colored men to load and unload vessels passing through the port of Galveston. Heretofore only white longshoremen had been employed on the wharves, and they had a monopoly of the steamship work. There was strong prejudice against Negro labor on the wharves and father, seeing the injustice of the situation, in spite of the strongest opposition and under most trying circumstances organized the men into an association of longshoremen. He purchased $2500 worth of tools and secured work on the Morgan wharf, paying the longshoremen $4 to $6 per day. It was not unexpected that any movement by which Negro labor would divide so lucrative an employment with the whites, should meet with fierce opposition. But in spite of the hostility toward his undertaking, father triumphed. He had secured laborers not only

42

in Galveston, but from New Orleans. The men were all skilled workmen.

Upon the question as to the difference in thoroughness between the white and colored labor, the following is one of many letters received by father from the shipmasters with whom he fulfilled contracts.

Dear Sir:—In reply to your question as to whether I am satisfied with the work you have on board my vessel, the *Jane,* I take pleasure in stating that my vessel has on board about 35,000 pounds more cotton than she took from New Orleans, and 75,000 pounds more than from Charleston, and I have these reasons for believing your work has been properly done. I shall, therefore, take pleasure in recommending you to any friends who may come here, believing as I do that you will conscientiously perform all you undertake to do, and that you will fully satisfy those who give you their confidence. I trust you will meet with the same success which has so far marked your path, and that my brother shipmasters will give you a full share of their patronage, seeing that in your undertaking you break down the very serious labor monopoly which has hitherto existed in this port to the great detriment of the shipping interests and indirectly the port itself.

Yours truly,

THOMAS ENGLAND.

After working for some time on the Morgan wharves, father attempted to secure contracts on the New York dock. This work was done altogether by whites. Not long after father's attempt, the white longshoremen launched a strike against the Mallory Steamship Company. Captain Sawyer of the Mallory Line called father in consultation with a view to engaging colored labor. Father promised to furnish the workmen, but stipulated that before doing so, he must have a guarantee that his men would not be "the catspaws to pull the chestnuts out of the fire." The condition was that the colored men would go to work, but must be retained on good behavior, and that in the future they were to have an equal showing with the white laborers. This promise was given and a rate of wages equal to that enforced on the Morgan wharf agreed upon.

The following morning, 9.30 o'clock, 110 of the colored cotton screwmen went to work discharging the steamship *State of Texas,* protected by a squad of police under Sergeant Connolly. The strikers were present, but they made no move to molest the men. Of course, the feeling was bitter against my father—the fiercest invectives were hurled against him and his life threatened. Always calm and cool in the face of danger, he continued with his brave workmen, his business on the steamship. Before the week ended, father came home one afternoon and, after greeting mother who was anxious and troubled, told her to take us (my baby brother Lloyd and myself) over to our Uncle Joseph Cuney's house and stay that night, for it was rumored in the town that a mob meant to visit our home and have his life. My mother flatly refused to leave the house. Putting my brother and me to bed, she took her vigil at a back window. Friends, a dozen or more, well armed gathered quietly at dark in the living room and dining-room, prepared to stay with father throughout the night and give him their protection.

In front of the house and across the street, hidden among the salt-cedars on the side-walks, were longshoremen—determined men, prepared to fight to the last, should the mob appear to lynch the man who was their leader and friend. Father begged mother to retire for rest but she was fearful that the mob might come from the back, through the alley-way and creep upon the men unawares, so all night long she sat at one of the windows at the back of the house, watching and fearing.

It was not until daybreak that it was learned that a number of the men had stationed themselves at both entrances to the back-way—they had taken every precaution not to be surprised by the mob—that no harm should come to the man who bravely faced all oposition for them.

Father's keen sense of right, his loyalty to the
best interests of his race, the utter fearlessness
which marked his conduct in this bitter contest
was not unappreciated by the equally fearless
men who followed him.   In order to be prepared
to meet any officers of the law who might come
upon them and try to disperse them, the men
had brought with them their guitars and other
stringed instruments, that they might claim a
"serenade" as an excuse for their loitering in
such numbers before our home.

The feeling was so intense that a number of
white citizens of importance, who had been
fairly disposed toward the colored workmen, had
also been threatened.   They were of that group
of splendid men of whom Galveston has always
boasted.   Their sympathy aroused such an-
tagonism that they were compelled to have
watchmen and officers protect their homes.   But
the anxious night passed safely.   My baby
brother and I could not understand our danger;
for mother, the night had been a hard and trying one.   But it had been made bearable by the
unpurchased watchfulness of that group of devoted men who stood by father in this grave
crisis.   For a number of days there were demonstrations of mob spirit, but it can be said to the
credit of Galveston that law prevailed.   The
strikers finally listened to reason, and the following report was published,—"Articles of capitu-

Lloyd Garrison Cuney

lation have been drawn up between the white strikers and the colored laborers who have been employed by the Mallory line to work in their places on the New York dock. The proposition from the committee representing the white laborers, is that there shall be a division of the work, with white and colored laborers working week in and week out upon the basis of two steamers to the week. The committee representing the colored screwmen have met this proposition with a response that they believe in an equal division of labor among all classes, and that no one class of labor should be employed to the exclusion or detriment of another. While they entertain these views, they do not consider that it is within their province or within the province of any labor element to dictate to Captain Sawyer, agent of the Mallory line, whom he shall employ, or map out for him any division of labor. They refer the whole matter to Captain Sawyer, and agree to abide by his decision. The report of the colored men shows upon its face the result of wise counsel. This report was submitted back to the white laborers yesterday, and will go to Captain Sawyer to-day." The result was that father's first agreement with the Mallory line was adhered to, and until to-day colored labor is employed on the Mallory wharves at Galveston.

CHAPTER VII.

FORGING TO THE FRONT, 1883–1884.

AT the close of the year 1883, civic affairs in Galveston became badly managed by the domination of rings. The better element of the city rebelled and decided to put forward a ticket presenting conscientious public men whose exertions they knew would be in the interest of good government. Father was persuaded to accept once more the nomination for alderman from the 12th ward for the years 1884 and 1885. Immediately opposition faced him, based on his conduct in the late strike. Flaming circulars and articles addressed "To the People" were printed. All bore an appeal to the prejudice of the narrow-minded and ignorant voter.

One article read—

"A very serious question is now before you— one involving the support of many white men and white families. R. L. Fulton, a candidate for Mayor, was a warm supporter of N. W. Cuney in a late contest. Not only Fulton but many of the present Board of Aldermen, were backers of N. W. Cuney in his attempt to re-

48

duce the price of the labor of cotton screwmen and longshoremen by importing from New Orleans, Negroes to be used as screwmen and longshoremen. Mr. Cuney did not enter the business with a view of gaining a livelihood; the first vessel he got he cut down the price per bale, thus showing that he was in favor of lowering wages. The white screwmen went on a strike. Did these people, or Capt. Fulton either, offer them any assistance or protection? No! On the contrary they aided and sustained Cuney, thus depriving white men of bread and meat. Have you forgotten this?

"Only a few days ago these same people aided in putting Mr. Cuney as a ruler over you. For the past two years, while R. L. Fulton has been acting Mayor, Cuney has been Mayor. Fulton never took a step without consulting Cuney, and if you elect Fulton and Cuney, Cuney will again be Mayor. It will not end here. Cuney is now in closer contact with his former friends, and in a position to make terms with them, and next Fall you will have five hundred Negroes screwing cotton, and your occupation will be gone. If you wish to have the heel of capital and the Negro upon your necks, vote for Fulton and elect him."

Thus ran the tirades, but, after a spirited contest, father was elected. The newly elected members of the City government succeeded in

breaking the "ring" and the commercial and
political interests were protected.

On the 20th day of March, a special meeting
of the City Council was called "to define the
functions of committees." This was occasioned
by a disagreement between the members of the
Committee on Hospital and Health. D. Fahey,
A. J. Musgrove and my father constituted this
Committee. The press had already learned of
their difference and articles had appeared under
the caption "Aldermanic wrangle." Mr. Musgrove, chairman of the Committee, reported to
the Galveston "Daily News" that the difficulty
had arisen over the selection of an overseer
of drays for the department of hospitals and
health. He stated that the morning after the
Mayor had announced his Committees to the
Council, he met Mr. Fahey on Mechanic Street,
and that the latter said to him—"You and
I are together on this committee; now let's ig-
nore this 'nigger' and run it ourselves," and
that he replied, "All right." They then discussed the naming of an overseer. This "understanding" between Mr. Musgrove and Mr. Fahey
led to a misunderstanding with my father, and
the Mayor called a special meeting to settle
the difficulty.

Two days later, on March 22d, father explained his attitude in an open letter to the
Galveston "News:" "That the people may be

thoroughly informed of the question involved in 'an aldermanic wrangle,' he said, "I ask the use of your columns to give them the true status of that part of our municipal affairs out of which the wrangle grew—caused in my opinion, by a careless disregard and want of appreciation of political duties on the part of the great mass of that element of our citizenship which neither seeks nor wants office, but which has a vital interest in a proper and economic administration of the city government. It does not become intelligent citizens to growl about bad government, when they show such a total want of patriotic appreciation of republican institutions, as to give themselves no concern about seeing to it that they have good government. If our government is bad, which I believe goes without saying, then I ask who is responsible, the men who administered it, or the men who allowed bad men to run it? This people can not have good government unless they deserve it, and they do not deserve it unless they make an honest effort by a faithful discharge of their public duties, to have it. If the city of Galveston were a private corporation and its citizens all stockholders, having their money invested, they would all be looking out for dividends and they would see to it that the directors whom they elected were men who would so conduct its business as to bring forth the dividend.

"The municipality of Galveston is a political corporation and every citizen is a stock-holder to the extent of his vote and the dividend this people ought to demand from those who are entrusted with the conduct of their business, is an honest and economical administration of government, courage in the assessment and collection of the revenues, and an honest and faithful expenditure, with a view to giving as many public improvements as possible after paying the necessary running expenses—a divorcement of the executive from the legislative branch, that each branch may more properly discharge its duties, thereby enabling the people to locate official responsibility.

"The real issue involved in this wrangle is whether the chairman of a committee of the city council shall be allowed to use his will and pleasure in contracting obligations, and generally to run the committee and the business in its hands to suit his gracious will and pleasure, or whether the majority of the committee shall direct how that portion of the public business referred to them shall be conducted. The position assumed by the chairman of the committee on hospitals and health is so absurd that no man who possesses any knowledge of republican institutions or parliamentary propriety would attempt to discuss it.

"The theory and practice of our government is that the majority and not the minority shall rule. I am clearly of the opinion that there is nothing in the charter nor in the ordinances giving committees power to employ men on what is generally known as corporation work. The engineer is the proper official to employ and discharge men in this department of the city government. With a view to having the duties and powers of the various committees defined, I, at the regular meeting of the city council held Oct. 15th, 1883, introduced and had referred to the committee on ordinances a resolution instructing that committee to report an ordinance defining the duties and powers of all committees. I hope this wrangle will be the means of straightening things out.

"When the chairman of the committee on hospital and health assumed the right to run the committee, the thought suggested itself to me, 'What are we here for?' I have no desire to wrangle, but my duty as an official trustee of the interest of this people is plain to me, and if an honest ambition to discharge my duty produces wrangling, then let those who attempt to exercise unlawful authority take the responsibility."

The year of 1884 was essentially one of politics. In the State campaign of this year, the Republicans desired to support Hon. George W. Jones for governor. There was some opposition to Mr. Jones, many being in favor of a straight ticket, but the real leaders of the party were in favor of him because it was believed that with him at the head of the ticket, there would be a chance of winning. There were extensive defections in the Democratic strongholds of the northwest portion of the state and it was possible for the majority to be dangerously reduced. The day before the convention convened at Houston a telegram was received from Col. Thomas P. Ochiltree declining to be a candidate for re-election to Congress. Col. Ochiltree was one of the picturesque figures in the state, as well known and as popular in New York as in Texas. He has facetiously been termed a compound of Beaconsfield, Sheridan and Falstaff. Noted for his good fellowship, he nevertheless relaxed no effort to subserve the interest of his commonwealth. His refusal to be again a candidate from the 7th Congressional district was received with regret.

The bill for the deepening of Galveston harbor was now before Congress. Friends of the measure, which was of all absorbing interest in Galveston, believed that Col. Ochiltree's continuance in office was essential to the success

of the bill.   The Republicans nominated Hon.
George B. Rentfro for Congress.   No one
supposed the opposition to Democracy would
determine the question of representation, but the
man most favorable to deep water and the
most efficient in aiding to secure it was the
one the independent voters of Galveston County
meant to support.

The Republican County Convention which
assembled April 3d, to elect delegates to the
State Convention, proved a signal victory for
father and his followers over the Malloy faction.   Failing to receive recognition as delegates, the opposing faction attempted to im-
pede the work of the convention, but father
was master of the situation.   Contesting delegations were sent to Fort Worth with Gen. Malloy at the head.   The local papers commented,
—"It is generally thought that owing to its
feebleness, it is the last expiring effort on the
part of the Malloy faction for party control
in this county.   The war has waged furiously
for many years, and the many political scalps
dangling from Mr. Cuney's belt proclaim the
completeness of his victory."   The fight was
carried to the convention which met the first
of May in Fort Worth.   Gen. Malloy was defeated and in an interview attributed his defeat to the fact that many white Republicans
voted, as they did, for father and the con-

vention recognized the Cuney faction as the
regular organization of Galveston County.
Forecasting the struggle at the National Convention, he added, "If Blaine men think the
majority of the successful delegation were for
Blaine, they are mistaken."

The convention at Fort Worth was called
to choose four delegates-at-large to the Republican National Convention which was to meet
at Chicago on the 3d of June. Gen. Malloy had
been a government official for many years and
a warm friend of Chester A. Arthur. He
fought for a unanimous delegation from
Texas for Arthur. My father, a strong Blaine
man, was selected delegate-at-large against his
protest. Following the convention the press
stated,—"Cuney was the only man who won a
victory; but Cuney's complexion precludes him
from leadership effectually. The day has not
yet arrived when a Negro can be the leader
of even the Republican party in Texas."

When the Texas delegation arrived in Chicago
early in June, there were already at the headquarters at the Sherman House, Colonel Patton,
who had at first gone to Washington, and Mr.
Webster Flanagan, straightforward in purpose,
and almost reckless in speech. Among the
Arthur leaders were Gen. Malloy, Col. De Gress
and Edward Burkett. Father was selected
member of the National Committee for the

state of Texas, and served in this capacity three consecutive terms. When the Convention assembled, the question of revising the representation at future national conventions started the first motion in the Texas delegation. Col. Nathan Patton moved to lay this motion on the table, but withdrew his motion to allow debate on the original. After a bitter fight made by the Southern members against the report, it was finally withdrawn amid cheers. The Convention was wild with enthusiasm for Blaine, but Texas had some extraordinary conversions for Arthur. This was met by a display of energy, fight and grand work for the Maine statesman. Father promised that Texas would give Blaine at the very least one-half of her twenty-six votes. The press reports stated: "N. W. Cuney, one of the most modest and yet one of the most solid in his influence in Chicago, is to-night working hard and effectively for Blaine. He has an up-hill task with the Texas delegation, for if Blaine gets more than five votes from Texas it will be due to Cuney's efficient management." Again it was said: "Cuney has handled the Blaine men with infinite tact; and held his thirteen solid in spite of blandishments of the Arthur men." During the balloting on the fourth day of the convention, the California delegates electrified the house with Webster Flanagan's cry—"What are

we here for?" The Texas delegation answered
the question on the first ballot by voting eleven
for Arthur, two for Logan and thirteen for
Blaine. On the last ballot Texas voted nine for
Arthur, sixteen for Blaine and one absent. The
ballot was completed and James G. Blaine, now
in full vigor of all his powers, was nominated
for the presidency.

The day before the Texas delegation left for
home, father found it necessary to defend himself from an attack made upon him. A special
dispatch to the Galveston "News," explains the
occurrence: "Chicago, June 8.—"Last night
there was a big sensation in the corridor of the
Sherman House. Bissell, formerly a customs
officer at Brazoria, and afterward editor of the
"Grand Army Gazette," at Washington, now
lives here. While in Texas he had several Republicans arrested for bull-dozing in Brazoria, but
the cases were dismissed by the United States
commissioner, there being no evidence whatever,
and Bissell acknowledged that he was mistaken.
Wright Cuney took a prominent part in the
defense of the accused, and when Bissell met
Cuney here he sought several opportunities to
create a difficulty with him, but the Galveston
representative treated him with contempt. Last
night Bissell with half a dozen Chicago hoodlums, sought Mr. Cuney in the Sherman House,
evidently determined on mischief, and they

found him—to their sorrow. Bissell approached
him and endeavored to start trouble, but Mr.
Cuney advised him to go away, turning con-
temptuously away from him. As he did so,
Bissell attempted to strike him with his cane,
when Cuney caught him quickly by the arm and
thrashed him unmercifully. Bissell finally
called for mercy and sneaked out of the hotel.
In five minutes all the Texas delegation were
around Mr. Cuney and it would have been
bad for any hoodlums attempting to interfere.
The Galveston representative has proved that
he is able to take his part, not only in politics,
but otherwise when necessary. All Texans here
are unanimously glad at Bissell's just punishment." A Democratic journal commented:
"N. W. Cuney's encounter in the rotunda of the
Sherman House shows he has pluck as well as
brains." At the close of the convention, father
was chosen one of a committee of fifty of its
members to notify Mr. Blaine officially of his
nomination, and arrived in Augusta, Maine, on
June 20.

An editorial from a Democratic journal read:
"A new element will hereafter be top rail in
the Texas Republican fence. It is headed by
Wright Cuney of Galveston—shrewd, untiring,
successful Cuney who held thirteen of the Texas
votes solid for Blaine. Malloy, Collector of
Customs at Galveston, headed the Arthur thir-

teen. It is said that thirteen is an unlucky
number. Cuney can afford to laugh at the super-
stition, but Malloy can't. It was a fair fight
between factions, each staking everything on the
result, and Cuney and his crowd have won.
Outside of the two gangs of Republicans there
could be no sympathy for either side, but
Cuney's plucky fight must perforce command
admiration. Verily it is a victory for Cuney."

The St. Louis Republic (Dem.) said: "N. W.
Cuney of Galveston, who spent several days
this week in St. Louis, is one of the ablest and
most influential men of African blood in the
South. He is the Texas member of the Republican National Committee, and carried a majority of the Texas delegation for Blaine in the
last Republican Convention, although every
custom house, post office and federal court building in the State was a recruiting agency for
Arthur."

Father, on his way home from the East, entered the Northern part of the State through
Texarkana. There he was questioned by a correspondent of the "Gazette," who published the
following: "As the southbound International
train rolled into the depot at Texarkana, the
eye of the 'Gazetteer' fell upon the spare form
of Wright Cuney, who is known to several
citizens of Galveston, especially to Gen. Malloy.
There is nothing in the personal appearance of

Cuney to indicate the many times the types have had of late to toy with his name in political connection. Slender figure, five feet, ten; straight black hair and mustache, black eyes; high cheek bones; a complexion more suggestive of Italy's sunny clime than of any portion of Africa's darkness; yet to-day he is the head and front of the Negro population of Texas. A representative man, well-informed, courteous, collected and with marked opinions on state and national politics. It may be possible that he has not modesty, but he well succeeds in assuming that virtue if he has it not. No one will detect any desire on his part to unduly push himself forward by other than legitimate means. Mr. Cuney has just returned from holding sweet communion with the man from Maine; having gone there with other delegates to inform Mr. Blaine of his nomination. 'We were splendidly entertained in Maine,' said Mr. Cuney, 'and our visit was made very agreeable. Of course you don't want me to recite the circumstances of our visit to Mr. Blaine's home; the press has already given that in full,' and he continued: 'Oh, of course we Republicans expect Blaine to be elected, and since my visit to New York I learned sufficient to show me that the Democrats can not carry that state. They will nominate Cleveland at Chicago. What do I expect for myself? Oh, nothing, nothing.

I am only a private citizen and have sought only to do my share in public matters toward my race and party. I am trying to build up my private business and expect to stick to that.' "

Father's reception on his return home was a most happy one. It was late in the afternoon when he reached home from his long journey, but we knew we were not to have him long to ourselves. Already before the train's arrival, men friends had come to the house and, taking possession of the yard, rapidly made preparations for the night's welcome. At dark, a procession of hundreds of torch-bearers, headed by a band, came marching down Avenue "L", awaking the streets and avenues with music and cheer. Father, with a few intimate friends, was called on the porch, while we sat at the windows that we might hear the speeches. After the serenading and speech-making, father gave an appreciative response.

The Galveston papers, though Democratic, were not remiss in showing pride in the honors bestowed upon their townsman; quoting the criticisms from the East, they headed their articles—"Our own and only N. W. Cuney." Among many interesting descriptions, was one from the New York Sunday "Press" of December 18,—"A bright, olive complexioned gentleman with a pleasant, clean cut face and a pair of eyes that look into one's soul; a well

made, self made man, full of native vigor and
the champion of his race in the far southwest;
brawny, active, well read on current topics and
an honor to the Republicans of Texas, N. W.
Cuney is one of the men that the new South, if
it ever exists, ought to cling to with clamps of
steel.   He lives down in Galveston, Texas and is
the Republican member of the National Committee from that State. A consistent and thoroughly
faithful man to his party, he has stood up for
its principles in the face of opposition that in
many other States of the South has made men
often silent—sometimes blind.   No Republican
is of better repute in the State—no one is more
popular even with his white fellow citizens than
the gentleman who yesterday started back to
Texas after being North at the meeting of the
National Committee."

CHAPTER VIII.

Alderman Cuney.

Early in the year 1885, after the defeat of Blaine, the Galveston city election was held and father for the third time became a candidate for Alderman on the Citizens' ticket. When the returns came in, Cuney, who had been duly elected, was counted out and C. J. Allen was said to be the successful candidate. Father knew that fraud existed and was determined to enter a contest. He had become a candidate this year representing the twelfth ward and the campaign had been one of close and intense interest, and the contest a notable one. The apparent irregularities in the returns from the eleventh ward formed the general subject of gossip, and the sentiment prevailed that the election returns had been tampered with, and fraudulent methods taken to defeat him.

Plans were instituted to contest the returns; affidavits were taken and a thorough canvass made. In the eleventh ward, the vote stood 309 for Allen and 21 for Cuney, against 162 in the tenth ward and 221 in the twelfth ward—contiguous wards. The total vote was 2389 for Cuney and 2492 for Allen. In the eleventh ward which was credited with 21 votes for father, 97 citizens made affidavit of having voted for him. In the meantime other affidavits were taken. More than 300 identified their ballots as having been changed. Many ballots were destroyed, and others substituted with Allen's name on them.

One of the prominent citizens who took the stand and swore that he had voted for N. W. Cuney and that the ballot had been changed, was Chief Justice A. H. Willie of the Supreme Court of Texas. Father, of course, won in the contest and on April 29th was declared elected. He was appointed on the Committees of Streets, Cemetery, Police and Markets.

In the City Council on April 19, 1886, Albert Weiss, Alderman, offered a resolution providing for the appointment by the Mayor, of a charter amendment committee. The resolution passed and the Mayor appointed from the Board of Aldermen, Albert Weiss, M. S. Kleberg and N. W. Cuney, together with three representative citizens and George P. Finlay, city attorney— the Mayor acting as ex-officio chairman. The Committee, after some weeks' session, suggested amendments to the city charter providing for the issuance of bonds for the construction of

a city hall and market house and for $200,000 to
be invested in street improvements and in the
water works. The decision of the Committee
caused considerable argument. One stubborn
point reached was the manner of electing aldermen—a matter which father moved to recon-
sider. It was moved to make six wards in the
city, one alderman to be elected from each
ward and in addition thereto, six aldermen to
be elected from the city at large. The question
was debated at length. Father favored the minority proposition, maintaining in his argument,
that by electing the entire body by the vote of the
whole city the virtual disfranchisement of the
minority would be achieved. The amendments
were finally passed.

The following year, he represented the city
as Alderman-at-large and was placed on two
of the most important committees, viz., the committee on finance and revenue, and the committee on claims and accounts.

This was an era marked by a growing tendency towards unfairness and humiliation for the
colored people. The South, interpreting the
law and the constitution according to her own
ideas of fairness, had not as yet found it necessary to make new laws in keeping with the
many acts of prejudice and discrimination.
Particularly were the railroads attempting to
discriminate against their colored passengers.

The case of Mrs. Morris, who had been forced into a second-class coach while holding a first-class ticket, engrossed father's attention and interest.

Another incident, amusing in some of its aspects, occurred about the same time and was one which touched him more closely. My uncle Joseph had gone to the depot with mother to see her off to Houston, where she was to join father, who was there attending a matter of business. The conductor of the first-class coach saw them coming and, knowing them to be colored, he quickly locked the door of the coach, as he knew from experience that no argument or force could compel mother to enter a second-class car. After locking the door he disappeared. It was then nearly train time and the coach was nearly filled with passengers. For a second, disconcerted, mother looked around and then innocently turning to Uncle Joseph, said: "Well, Joe, there are people in the coach and I see but one means of entrance and that is the window, so give me your hand as a mount." And then, as if mounting a horse, she got in the window and took her seat demurely. It was now time for the train to leave, so the conductor hastened forward, glanced hastily around, saw only Uncle Joseph and surmising that his strategy had worked, unlocked the door

and cried with great satisfaction, "All aboard."
Entering his coach to collect tickets he was
greatly chagrined and bewildered to see mother
sitting there quite contented and with perfect
ease and indifference.

CHAPTER IX.

THE THICK OF THE FIGHT.

ON the first of December, 1886, in the town of Brenham, three Negroes were taken from the jail and hung. Newspaper reports read: "The mob was composed of from twenty to sixty men, quiet, sober and well-behaved. They came to town on business and their plans had been carefully prepared and they were carried out to the letter."

There had been election disturbances in the county for two years previous to the lynching. At a general election, a number of armed men, masked, entered the election room in the nearby town of Chappel Hill, and without a word of warning shot three colored men who were engaged in counting the vote, without even a following investigation or arrest. The memory of this outrage caused the colored people to be watchful and ready to defend themselves and their franchise.

In the Fall election which followed, 475 legal Republican ballots were seized and destroyed by armed masked men, while boxes of returns were destroyed. Bolton, said to be a prominent citizen, was among the masked men engaged in seizing the ballot and was killed.

The Negroes who were lynched, with five others, were charged with having been implicated in the murder. The men were released under bonds. Acting under advice of friends, they refused to accept the release. Eight colored men who were present at the time Bolton was killed were arrested by a large force of armed men and kept in custody near Brenham.

Immediately afterwards, the Commissioner's Court met and declared the election of all candidates on the "People's" ticket. At the same time a cry was raised of Negro insurrection. A telegram was sent to the sheriff for the purpose of getting him away from the city. Crowds of excited men gathered—mutterings concerning Negro supremacy were heard, and open threats made.

The "Radicals" made incendiary speeches and blamed the Republicans for the disturbances, saying they had used whiskey and money to secure the Negro vote and had favored "social equality." Advantage was taken of the death of Bolton to stir up popular prejudice and to foment mob violence, which finally culminated in the wholesale hanging of the defenseless colored prisoners.

Brenham boasts a fine German population and

German citizens compose the property owners of the county. They were nearly all Republicans and were, as they are to-day, peaceably disposed citizens. They condemned the lynching which disgraced their town. One citizen stated, "these colored men were taken from jail and hung not because they were guilty of crime, but because they knew too much about the crimes of the men who were the instigators of the lynching."

At a meeting over which father presided, resolutions were framed "condemning such acts of lawlessness, calling attention to the dilatory action of the Governor during the labor troubles and his promptness in sending troops to quell imaginary Negro uprisings."

Father both wrote and spoke against the action of the cowardly mob, which caused him to be the recipient of anonymous letters. One of Dec. 8th, read: "Come up here—we have fifty men who can clean you up. We know you and you had better look out. We are more than anxious for the blood of such stirrers-up of race prejudice. We would like very well to see you and beg you to come up here and help the cause of your brother murderers.

(Signed) "Revenge."

No action was taken by the authorities to apprehend the lynchers but the outrage rankled in the heart of every colored man in the State.

Shortly after father received the anonymous letters, my mother and I passed through Brenham en route to Austin. Father, who accompanied us, had telegraphed Brenham friends to meet him at the train, as it stopped for twenty minutes at that station—his customary way, when traveling, of seeing his political friends.

I well remember my mother pleading with him not to go out on the platform for fear he would be harmed. He laughed her fears aside and, declaring "they are all cowards," swung down from the train steps and talked with his friends until the time for departure.

The following year, father for the fifth time was a candidate for the city council on the "Citizens'" ticket. The Galveston Tribune in an interview with one of the leading merchants of Galveston, was told: "I hear that there is a disposition in some quarters to scratch Mr. Cuney, but it will not be sufficient to defeat him.

"It is mainly race prejudice, but it is confined to a very few people. The colored people are among us and they are certainly entitled to representation. It is estimated that there are 5000 colored people in Galveston. It is a credit to both races that a man of Mr. Cuney's ability has been so often chosen to represent not alone these 5000 people, but the people at large.

"A short time since, I overheard Captain Jim

McDonald express his opinion of Mr. Cuney. When Capt. McDonald went into the council, he was very prejudiced against him, but after having been associated with him for two years as a member of the city council, he frankly admitted that he was an able and conscientious representative and that no man could impugn his honesty. No man will question Capt. McDonald's candor, for he has the courage to avow his convictions. It is also asserted that there is dissatisfaction with Mr. Cuney among his own people, but I think the amount of this dissatisfaction is too small to talk about. Mr. Cuney will get the solid support of the best citizens. He has made a good representative and he should be re-elected."

In opposition to Mayor R. L. Fulton, Col. McAlpine had entered the field for Mayor. The men who were managing the McAlpine candidacy were determined to win and planned to cut the "Citizens'" ticket all along, unless the "Citizens'" Committee joined in the gas company's fight against Fulton.

It was reported: "What is known as the 'rule or ruin element,' in all emergencies join hands with that element typified as hoodlumism. It is well known that this crowd does not want McAlpine, but they do want to defeat Fulton. They are willing to sacrifice the "Citizens'" ticket—

willing to sacrifice the best interests of the city
to get even with Fulton."

The followers of both McAlpine and Malloy
scratched the "Citizens'" ticket in the interest
of their respective candidates. The plan was
to sacrifice a vote for alderman for a vote for
Mayor and to promise a number of votes for
the "Citizens'" ticket, provided they would deliver a like number of votes for Malloy.

Father was the victim of this combine. The
McAlpine managers cast the white vote almost
solidly for his opponent, Allen. They had failed
to influence the colored voters. It was suspected
that a quiet understanding had been arrived
at among the McAlpinites to sacrifice Cuney
and steps were taken to verify it. Men were
placed at several polling places to note the
counting. The listeners noted every ticket that
McAlpine headed and the names for aldermen
as they were called off. The McAlpine supporters voted the "Citizens'" ticket straight with
the one exception, Allen.

The Galveston daily papers commented upon
my father's defeat with regret. A Houston
Herald editorial read: "N. W. Cuney and
the paragrapher of the Galveston Evening
Tribune should be tied together for some time.
The Tribune weeps because Cuney wasn't elected
over a good white Democrat."

The reply came: "The Tribune paragrapher

would rather be tied to a brainy colored man than to a fledgling journalist who hasn't discretion enough to keep quiet regarding matters of which he absolutely knows nothing."

The Houston Post, a daily that fought father for many years, commented: "They downed the Negro politician, Wright Cuney, in the Galveston city election. The good things come in small streaks this year."

Again the Galveston paper retorted. "The streak was so small that time that a majority of the intelligent people of Galveston failed to see it. Wright Cuney made an excellent alderman and would have been re-elected had he consented to sacrifice another (Fulton) to save himself—had he consented to use his influence to induce colored men to sell their votes. Cuney refused to do this and the men who made the proposition, carried out their threat and knifed him. Wright Cuney, the Negro politician, would rather be right and retain his self-respect than crawl into office through treachery and corruption."

After the election, father was appointed by the newly-elected Mayor, Mr. Fulton, and confirmed by the city council, as a member of the Board of Commissioners of Water Works. He served as commissioner for two years, 1887-1889. The water works, including the collection of water rates, tolls and revenues, were under the control and management of the Board of Commissioners, while it was also their duty to appoint all officers, agents and employés necessary for the operation of the works.

The twentieth legislature by special act gave Galveston authority to issue $450,000 in bonds for the construction of a water works system. "Too much praise," it was said, "cannot be given to Messrs. Brown, Beers, Crooks and Cuney, for their labor in bringing about such excellent results."

During the anti-prohibition campaign in May 1887, the Dallas anti-prohibition convention named my father as one of the sixty-two members of the Executive Committee for the State. He declined to serve, giving the reason that he was a member of the National Republican Executive Committee, and to accept such a position might be construed as giving the anti-prohibition movement a political recognition and sanction which had so far been avoided on both sides. The prohibition question was submitted to the people at a time when no general election was to be held, for the express purpose of giving the voter an opportunity of deciding without making it a "party" question. Party leaders disagreed as to the effect the prohibition movement had upon the Republican party in the State.

Father, when questioned, replied in a letter

to the Ft. Worth Gazette of Sept. 12th: "The effect of the prohibition canvasses upon the future of the Republican party in this State is almost wholly conditioned upon the future action of the Democratic party in reference to the disposal of that vexatious question.

"The prohibition was, to the Republicans, a 'go-as-you-please.' I think it is a fact, that cannot well be controverted, that fully one-third of them voted the anti ticket. Should the Democratic party in its convention next year declare prohibition un-Democratic, it will be offensive to many prohibition Democrats. But they will not for that reason join the Republican party.

"They would become out-and-out prohibitionists, were it not for fear that such action might in some way aid the Republican party. This in their minds is a greater evil than whiskey. This is especially true in all Southern States, except those that are developing their mining and manufacturing interests.

"Should the Republican party declare for prohibition, it would cost the loss of the German vote; they would not gain the Democratic Prohibitionists, for outside of a few centers of population, our Southern Democrats are Bourbons and don't intend that any prohibition or labor movement shall be their 'Trojan horse.' "

When asked, at the same time, concerning

the tariff, he continued: "I think it is plain to any observer of current politics, that the tariff question, in so far as it relates to labor, has placed our Democratic friends in Virginia and Tennessee in the condition of most people when they go to sea.

"Mr. Mills may cry out from the wilderness that Mr. Randall 'must go,' but he will find that the next national platform of his party will have in it a double ender—upon one end he will find Mr. Randall and his protection friends and upon the other, Messrs. Carlisle, Morrison, Madison and himself; leaving it to Mr. Randall and his friends, to say to the manufacturing interests that it means protection, and the others to say to the rural and shipping interests that it means free trade."

CHAPTER X.

HOME LIFE.

THE twelfth ward in Galveston, in which we always lived, was in the East End of the city, near the beach. Our house, which was a modest one, was in every sense a home.

My mother was not strong and spent much time out doors with her flowers. There were roses—red, pink and white, and the yellow Marechal Neil; borders of violets, daffodils and jonquils in the spring, and asters and chrysanthemums in the fall, with cape jasmine, well known in Texas, but now rare and precious to me, after years of life in the Northeast.

Back of the house were orange trees, plum and pomegranate, the purple fig and mulberry trees, where we used to read perched upon seats among the branches. Mother cared zealously for her flowers until Easter, when the yard, awakened by the spring, would be stripped and the flowers carried to the hospital.

Our home life was particularly happy. The three married brothers lived within a radius of three blocks. There were seven cousins, and as

we were near the same age, we were companion-
able and always warm friends. We found much
pleasure on the beach and in the surf. Father,
who enjoyed surf bathing, went often with us.

Christmas and New Years were of course
our gayest holidays. There was always a generous Santa Claus, but father gave his personal
gifts on the first day of the year. The night
before, we always had a family party enlivened
by the visits of intimate friends. Father enjoyed reading aloud the poems of the old year,
always closing with "Ring out the old, ring in
the new." As midnight approached, we would
guess the minute and all troop out doors to
see the stars shining on the new-old world.

"Open house" was held on New Years Day,
with the reception for the grown-ups.

Christmas with the children's party and the
candle-lighted tree, always brought us books
galore. Our first introduction to New England
was through a treasured Christmas book—"A
Family Flight Around Home," by Edward
Everett Hale and his sister.

Father cared but little for current fiction.
He read deeply, preferring early Hebrew, Greek
and Roman history. He was fond of the
classics, and in poetry, enjoyed Byron, perhaps
next to Shakespeare. He often read aloud to
us, and we liked to listen, although there were
many things which we could not understand.

Shakespeare was his beloved poet, and he knew him intimately. Father's enthusiasm awakened the interest of my boy cousins, and the two brothers, Richard and Wright, who bore my father's name, used to commit to memory long passages, and in the dining room made cheerful by an open fire, they rehearsed scenes from Shakespeare's plays. We young children of the family, Nisi, Philip, Daisy, my brother Lloyd and I, composed the audience and thought the actors very wonderful.

A retainer and faithful friend of ours limped in his walk. Father said he walked like Richard III, and often when this man came into his presence, would softly quote in an affectionate, quizzing undertone, passages from the play.

Father, intensely sympathetic and generous to a fault, was often imposed upon. Mother continually reprimanded him for going on bond for some repentant law-breaker, who had pleaded for a chance to reform and, usually, to run away; or for bestirring himself to get work for some unfortunate who repaid him by opposing him in the next election.

There were certain men in Galveston who invariably opposed him in any convention, or in any of his public undertakings, but who came to him whenever they were out of work. Mother argued against his assisting them, but in spite of the fact that his kindness was abused, he was not soured. He met every argument smilingly and repeated the phrase: "Forgive them, they know not what they do."

He had a hatred of form and ceremony and was impatient with creed and dogma. While he belonged to no church, he had the heart and soul of a Christian, and was a follower of the Lowly Nazarene.

The term "Nigger" was hateful in the extreme to father and was never used in our home. Upon one occasion, when we attended the theatre in Boston to see the Kendalls—(he never entered a theatre in the South)—father was incensed at Mr. Kendall's free use of the word Nigger on the stage, and both the play and the English actor were lowered in his estimation.

Our home was a music-loving one. Mother played the piano and sang. Father's appreciation was not that of the ultra-modern school. He liked the old songs of Ireland, martial strains and melodies from the old Italian operas.

The correction of our childish faults lay chiefly in mother's hands, for father could not withstand tears or pleadings. However, he taught us self-control and always cautioned my brother and me, to "Do as you please, but please to do right." He was particularly sensitive and tender in his affections. No wish of mine was ever left ungratified, and nothing would put him in a more furious rage than any question of my ill treatment. It was so in later years. He remained my worshipping and worshipped father.

Little time did he give to pleasure, for life took a strong hold on him. He continually shortened his sleeping hours in order to have more time for his work—an unfortunate habit, for he early suffered from insomnia; a condition due, no doubt, to overwork, and his nervous desire to lengthen his working day. Aside from his private business, in his work for better racial conditions, the demands on his time were enormous. He was no "holiday politician" and, imperious and impetuous as he was in action, he fought his battles with sincerity and earnestness.

At three o'clock father was usually at home, unless detained on one of the ships that the longshore men might be loading far out in the harbor. The close of the dinner hour was one of the happiest periods of the day. Father, sipping his claret, his only dinner wine, followed by the inevitable cigar—he smoked incessantly —would in these moments of leisure, talk of the world happenings of the day, or engage in discussion with mother over some book they were reading. I remember particularly their talk of Mrs. Ward's Robert Elsmere.

CHAPTER XI.

FORT BEND.

ONE afternoon in the late Fall of 1888, father was not at home at the expected time and mother, thinking he was detained by business, decided not to delay the dinner hour. We were in the dining room when father came into the house. His face was wan and he looked weary. Mother, quick to notice the slightest change in his countenance, questioned him. Unable to reply, he sat down at the table and buried his head upon his arms. He was thoroughly disheartened and unnerved.

Finally he told us what had happened. Fort Bend county, the heart of the black belt, where colored men had worked long and well, and had acquired valuable lands and money, was in the hands of a rioting white mob, and well-known colored men had been persecuted.

There had been two recent murders in the county. On was that of R. L. Shamblin, a prominent citizen of Richmond, who while sitting in his home reading out of the Bible to his family, was fired upon from without and killed. The other was that of Henry Frost, who was fired upon from ambush. The two men were white Democratic leaders of the disturbing faction known as the "Jaybirds."

Without investigation, colored men were said to be "agitators" and "suspected" of having instigated the assassinations. The result was that six of the most prominent colored citizens—intelligent men who held important offices—were driven out of the county. Charles M. Ferguson, district clerk, and Dr. Davis, a well-known physician, were given forty-eight hours to leave. No opportunity was given them to provide for the safety of their families or to dispose of their property. Wm. Caldwell, another colored citizen, was arrested for the killing of Shamblin.

Organized mobs took possession of the towns and thoroughly intimidated the colored people who remained. An appeal was made to Gov. Ross, who sent the Adjutant General to the scene. This officer refused to confer with the sheriff, but consulted the mob instead, remarking that the next time he came, it would not be as an official, but that he would help kill every Negro in the county.

A number of the men father knew personally. He heard that they were forced to flee, leaving their families to face the mob. He was greatly grieved and wanted to take immediate action to help his friends. Mother tried to console him and told him that whatever action he might take would only lead to danger for himself, and perhaps (prophetically speaking), would be repaid by the enmity of the very men for whose misfortune he now grieved.

This was a new scene in our happy home life, and for the first time I realized what the word "prejudice" meant. Father had repeatedly taught us that "all men were equal," but this seemed a dark horror that could not be reasoned away.

After the riot appeared a new publication calling itself "The Official Organ of the Jaybird Democratic Association of Fort Bend County." One editorial said: "Fort Bend, Waller, Brazoria, Wharton and Matagorda have long been known as the Senegambian districts, and have suffered no little from designing politicians followed by the vast ignorant Negro population, but the white citizens at last got their eyes open, and we now expect to see a radical change in the political standing of these counties, and that too in a very short time. Fort Bend Democrats have just succeeded in freeing themselves from Negro rule and are now willing to aid other counties in doing the same."

In November, an effort was made to conciliate the frightened Negroes. A notice was published to the effect that a mass meeting would be held at the Court House, with a view to explain that the object of the recent Democratic association was not to disfranchise the Negro altogether!

"The White Man's Union," another association organized the same month, held a convention and from their platform gave more light as to the cause of the recent race riot. They stated that "the feeling had been intense over the election of a Negro, last Fall, to the office of county and dristict clerk and our object was to discourage Negroes from filling public offices." Their influence was so strongly felt, that it resulted in the resignation of the county clerk and colored constable. "Resignations were accepted!" A new clerk and constable, both white, immediately took the oath and much satisfaction was expressed.

The Fort Bend County Grand Jury returned two indictments against Mr. Ferguson, one charging him with being an accessory to the assassination of Shamblin, and the other, with conspiring to assassinate Frost. Forced to leave his family and home, Mr. Ferguson went to Nashville, Tenn., hoping to file a suit in the Federal Courts against forty citizens of Fort Bend County. Later, he went to Washington, D. C., to seek government employment.

Father took charge of his interests, and on Sept. 28th, he wrote to Hon. George C. Tichenor at Washington: "I desire to repeat what I said to you while in Washington, regarding the appointment of Mr. Ferguson to the position which he seeks as one fraught with great importance to the Republicans, not only of Texas, but throughout the South. Outside of the fact that he is honest, intelligent and worthy to fill the position, he has claims upon a Republican administration.

"We propose to make a test case of his suit, as to whether a man can be driven from his home and his property, by the oligarchy which not only now rules the South, but proposes to rule the country—because he dares to differ with it on political questions. I enclose herewith a copy of his petition filed in the U. S. Court here, that you may better understand just what we are striving to accomplish in this case. I hope you will have time to read it and lay the same before the Secretary.

"It does seem to me that our friends in the North are asleep on this Southern question. They have not the time to consider it or they certainly would understand the purposes of this southern oligarchy. The South has ceased to be a democracy so far as the Negro is concerned. I urgently recommend that immediate action be taken in this case."

In a letter to Hon. J. S. Clarkson, then First Assistant Postmaster General, he said: "My friend, Mr. Ferguson, will call on you to talk about a matter of vast importance not only to himself, but to southern Republicans in general. I hope you will spare him as much time as possible and be patient to listen to what he has to say.

"When you thoroughly understand his case, I know that you will be deeply interested in it and will do what you can to aid him. I was assured while at Washington that he would be given a position as special inspector of Customs at some point outside of Texas. A few days before leaving, I had a long interview with Secretary Windom, explaining to him fully the situation in this case. Mr. Tichenor recommended to the Secretary that he be appointed, but there seems to be a hitch somewhere."

About the same time father wrote to David Abner, Jr., who is now the President of Conroe College, Texas:

"I write you in the interest of Mr. Charles M. Ferguson, who you know was driven from his home by a Democratic mob at Richmond some time since. You are doubtless aware of the fact that he is now at Nashville, Tenn., to which place he has taken his family, thus enabling him to bring a suit in the Federal Court against those who drove him away from his home and property. There has been employed one of the strongest firms of lawyers in the State, to prosecute his suit, and they are more than sanguine of success. The case has been set down for the November term at Galveston.

"His enemies in Fort Bend County have indicted him on several counts with a view of forestalling him in his suit against them here. This move is understood thoroughly ·by his lawyers and friends here. This, in my judgment, will be one of the most remarkable cases in the history of our courts, and one in which every manly Negro should feel a deep interest. You know that a prosecution of this kind cannot be carried on without money. It is of the highest importance to a successful issue that we should raise a few hundred dollars.

"I understand that he is a high official in the order of Odd Fellows, of which you are the head in the State. I also understand that the Order is in a flourishing condition. This being the case, I think an assessment of about five dollars per lodge, with what his personal and masonic friends will raise, will give us a fund amply sufficient for all purposes.

"I sincerely hope that you will go to work at once in this matter and forward your collection to Mr. Trowell or to me, as you see fit. Let me hear from you at once as to what you can do or will do, for the time is short and this money must be raised."

The matter was taken up by Mr. Abner and others, and on Dec. 13th, father wrote to friends:

"C. M. Ferguson arrived here on Saturday night. He went to jail Wednesday afternoon, sued out a writ of habeas corpus and was released on $2700. His matters are in good shape and I do not think there is any doubt as to a judgment in his favor."

Upon his arrival in Galveston, Mr. Ferguson came directly to our home. It was thought best to take precautions for his personal safety, and that night he was taken to the home of my father's brother, Joseph. Here for four days he remained unseen except by the most intimate friends. On December eleventh, he voluntarily surrendered himself to the authorities.

Under the Civil Rights Act, the United States grand jury indicted sixty-two citizens of Fort Bend County, including the sheriff and county attorney, for forcing the colored men to leave their homes, and there was also an indictment by the same jury of twenty-six citizens of Richmond, charged with murder growing out of the Richmond riot.

Mr. Ferguson's suit called for $55,000 damages. The trial was held in Galveston County. The result was that the cases were dismissed at the cost of the defendants, a compromise having been effected whereby Ferguson was awarded $9,000 and $1,000 was received by Dr. Davis.

CHAPTER XII.

THE "LILY WHITES."

"RIOTS" and "Race wars" such as had disgraced the counties of Fort Bend and Wharton and deeply injured their citizens, were traceable to the displeasure of the ambitious white office seekers.

Political aspirants within the Republican party felt that the Negro was taking too prominent a part in the affairs of government. The State convention of 1884 had demonstrated their purpose of expelling the colored American from the party, if possible, and now the mask was completely thrown aside.

The first step was to overthrow the recognized leader, Cuney, and strip him of his power and influence. The fight in favor of southern prejudice could not be won as long as a Negro with his following of black voters stood at the head of the party in Texas.

The building up of a white man's Republican party in the South was however impossible. The Negroes of the South could not be wrongfully used without offending their brothers in the

92

North, and had it not been for the Negro vote,
Ohio, Illinois, Indiana and perhaps New York
would have been overwhelmingly Democratic.
However, in 1888, the struggle was begun
by the organization of "white Republican clubs,"
for the purpose of controlling the county conventions that they might elect their delegates
for the State conventions. Father sarcastically
referred to the instigators of a "white Republican party" as the "Lily Republicans" and the
"Lily Whites."

In the Chicago Inter Ocean, Mr. Albion Tour-
gée wrote: "The Colored Republican party of
Texas have manifested an aptitude for political
warfare which goes far to disprove the allega-
tion of inferiority, by dubbing the so-called
white Republicans who recently met, 'Lily
White.' The name is a good one and all the
more stirringly appropriate, for as everybody
knows, that faction thus arrogating to itself
purity, capacity and patriotism, is organized for
plunder, under the leadership of one whose open
debasement of Republican principles has become National. The pure-minded patriot of
'Flanigan's Mills' is a fit standard bearer for
the 'Lily Republicans' who wish to cut the party
loose from the Negro in order that they may
control whatever plums of Federal patronage
and representative power may fall to the party
organization of the Lone Star State."

At the Galveston County Convention of April
3d, which was held in pursuance of a call of
the Chairman of the County Republican Executive Committee, for the purpose of selecting
delegates to the State Republican Convention
which was to meet at Fort Worth in September,
father, who had been selected as a delegate, was
called upon to address the meeting. He spoke
with no bridled tongue of the political outrages in Arkansas and Fort Bend County, Texas,
and further stated that he recognized the fight
was on to overthrow the Negro Republicans in
the State, and characterized the promoters of the
warfare as thieves and pickpockets. He asked
no quarter in the coming struggle and would
give none.

The White Republicans, angered, attempted
to influence the colored delegates to split on the
color question. It was their object to create
a factional fight among the colored men, so that
they would be free from blame. Their main
fight was centered on the chairmanship of the
convention, placing Louis Johnson against Ed.
Davis, who was proposed by the Cuneyites for
the position. The Cuney element won, and the
delegation was equally divided among the white
and colored.

In a report of the proceedings, especial stress
was laid upon father's denunciation of the riot-
ers in the State. A prominent Galveston citi-

zen, J. B. Stubbs, writing an open letter to the Galveston News, said: "It is just such inflammatory speeches as that delivered by Mr. Cuney last night that incites Negroes when in the majority to domineer over their white neighbors until the latter rise to either precipitate bloodshed or force them to leave. . . . I am surprised at Mr. Cuney. He is a man of intelligence and has been the recipient of many honors at the hands of the people of this city; yet one would think from his speech that Negroes were not safe in Texas."

A San Antonio daily was of the opinion: "While Mr. Cuney might be termed a rabid partisan, few who know him will question that his utterances come from the heart—that he voiced his earnest conviction."

The State Convention was held at Fort Worth on September 19th. Terribly in earnest, the men assembled on the question of nomination or no nomination for the coming gubernatorial contest. But the question was something more than party success in the coming election; there were the well laid schemes to draw the color line, by a number of white Republicans, which the colored voters were determined to defeat. On the scene were Rosenthal, Newcomb, Spaulding and dozens of white Republicans from North and South Texas, who came to fight for the nomination of a State ticket, claiming that failure to do so would be an intimation that the Republicans were afraid to place a State ticket in the field—and announcement that property and life were unsafe in Texas and that the laws did not protect either.

On the other hand, the "no-nominating" element gave strong and cogent reasons for their position. They claimed that many Republicans who before voted for Blaine were with the Union Labor people. The election of the Republican State ticket being impossible, they would be free to trade with the Martin men and thus secure for Harrison a greater strength than Blaine had in 1884. They did not state that there was physical danger in nominating a ticket, but declared that the failure to do so was best for the Republican party as a National party.

Malloy, Cochran, Millet, McCormack and Cuney led the anti-ticket men; De Gress, Newcomb, Rosenthal and perhaps a majority of the white delegates were ranged on the side of De Gress, who called the Convention to order September 20th.

In his address to the Convention, placing John T. Brady of Harris County in nomination for temporary chairman, father mentioned interviews and opinions given by certain members of the Convention. If quoted aright, they had come there to draw the color line. They meant to put him in the attitude of one who would

for political purposes, misrepresent his home—
the State of Texas.

The effect of his speech was to anticipate
the issue and there was much confusion. Major
De Gress abandoned the chair to Robinson and
took the floor to make personal explanation. He
said the representative of the St. Louis Globe
Democrat asked him what he thought of the
troubles in Fort Bend County, and that he replied that he knew nothing of them, but was
not surprised as he had been told that trouble
was expected.

Rosenthal rose to explain that he was not
drawing the color line, but repeated on the floor
of the Convention what he had said on the
outside, that life and property were safe in
Texas. He had stated this to Northern capitalists and was not prepared to stand before them
now and say he was guilty of falsehood.

When Lock McDaniel remarked: "In Grimes
County every man was as free from danger and
intimidation as at any place on God's earth,"
J. M. Snider of Travis asked: "Why then were
the Sheriff and Deputy Sheriff of that county
assassinated?" For the moment yells prevented
McDaniel from answering.

James P. Newcomb stated that he was one
of the men reported as having been interviewed
and charged Cuney himself with drawing the
color line. He said that he deprecated the draw-

ing of it, but if it was drawn, it was drawn forever.

Thus the controversy waged until father took the floor. The scene was thus reported: "As N. W. Cuney took the floor a heavy rain came up, the lightning flashed and thunder rolled. Something was expected from Cuney and the situation was strained. Cuney could not, at first, be heard on the platform, but his manner and the elements for the first time during the Convention secured a silence that was almost oppressive after the jamboree that had lasted for hours.

"He walked up and down the aisle. His step is smooth and cat-like, his voice is soft and melodious and then again stern and harsh. His gestures are graceful and his language far above the average, but his power is in the fact that he feels his strength. He knows it. His speech was at first an explanation of his position. It was simply that he was a Republican and a Texan. He dared to point out where the Democrats had dealt unjustly by his race, but in doing it he did not assail his mother State. No man could teach him. He had held offices of trust and emolument. He called on good men, Democrats as well as Republicans, to say whether or not he had been a clean servant. He had been charged by the Democratic press with being a leader of a faction. This was false.

"He knew no color in Republicanism, but fought for it without scrutinizing the complexion of the men who stood beside him in the ranks. After he was done with this line, he lectured the element of the party that were dissatisfied with the present state of affairs. He had taken the stand by this time. He walked before the footlights. He spoke kindly—he spoke severely. He pleaded for harmony—he scowled and shook his finger. It was a sight worth seeing. He trod the boards like a Booth. He was the actor with his part well in hand, the master spirit that knows that what he says is treasured and not to be soon forgotten . . . it was a climax, so delivered that his followers took fire and he swept all before him from that time on."

When the vote was taken for temporary chairman father's candidate, Grady, was elected. J. E. Wiley of Dallas was elected Secretary and William Edgar Easton of Travis, assistant Secretary. After an excited controversy, the "no-ticket" men won, and after a lengthy and heated debate, the report of the committee on platform and resolutions was adopted. The resolutions ratifying the nomination of Harrison and Morton demanded such national legislation as would give adequate protection to wool, hide and other Texas products and industries, and denounced the Fort Bend and Washington County outrages.

After the adjournment of the Convention there was a caucus held by those who were indignant at the alleged arbitrary actions of the chairman. But wise counsel prevailed and, though the indignation remained, the caucus voted down every motion for the publication of a protest, or the encouragement of anything like rebellion from the action of the Convention.

Thus the first attempt to draw the color line in the Republican party in Texas was defeated, but it called forth bitter criticism. An article which appeared in the daily press under the caption "The State's Traducers" scored the victorious "no-party" element in the Convention. Part of it follows: "Such open bulldozing has never been seen in Convention in Texas. The resolutions denouncing the Fort Bend and Washington County troubles were drawn with all the skill and cunning of a Macchiavelli. They were not, by themselves, an arraignment of either party, but their framers well knew that the State's enemies at the North would seize upon them with the stories of fraud and force already published, and with the refusal to nominate a ticket, thus weave them into a reign of terror in Texas, in which the life of a Republican was always in danger and the ballot in the hands of a Negro a mere farce.

"Of course it is asking a good deal of a man who has maintained his self-respect to mix with such people as were the controlling spirits in the recent Republican gathering in Fort Worth. An aspirant for congressional honor allowed himself to be made a puppet in the hands of Wright Cuney, a man with intelligence enough to lay his plans, but too much regard for his own dignity to carry them out. . . . Let this band who furnished the enemies of Texas with grounds for their calumnies be held up to the scorn and derision of the people throughout the Union, until their names shall become a hissing and reproach in the mouths of honest men—let them be denounced from every newspaper and pilloried in every county in the State."

During the campaign, one of the most bitter appeals made to prejudice, was that of Hon. A. W. Terrell at a large Democratic rally held November 4, 1889. After an exposition of Democratic doctrines and the canvass for deep water in the Galveston harbor, he said: "What assurance have you that our Democratic senators and congressmen from Texas might not inspire your engineers to hunt for deep water elsewhere when you have rebuked them by injecting Brewster with Cuney into their counsels? With Brewster in Congress elevated on a platform made of the mixed wool of the merino and the

African, with Cuney as Postmaster and some
other saddle-colored political saint in the Custom
House, I say if those things are to be the reward for Crain's fidelity to his whole district,
it would be a just retribution to see your Democratic congressman whispering into the ears of
the engineers to search cautiously for deep
water elsewhere. . . . And who is Cuney? Once
respected as an intelligent mulatto, he forfeited
your respect when he charged that the good
people of Washington and Fort Bend Counties
would not permit a free ballot to Negroes. The
slander of our people in this crisis of their
fate should consign him to infamy.—The foremost man of all the world is the Anglo-Saxon
American white man. By the ties of a common
blood, higher than party and party policies, I
appeal to you to quit the ranks of the black
cohorts, who, by their race hatred and ingratitude, now jeopardize social order and property
rights. Their depraved leaders have magnified
every individual wrong done to a Negro, into a
sectional grievance and cause our people to be
misunderstood and hated throughout the North.
Cuney has been petted too long by the Galveston people. When he charged that martial
law was desirable to the present condition of
affairs, and prated upon the insecurity of the
colored people in certain sections of this State,
it was simply a bait thrown out to Northern

Republicans for bloody shirt purposes. It was a pretty picture, this African leader pulling the white Republicans of the State around by the nose, leading them off after Marion Martin and the new-fangled Labor Union party, while he went about slandering the people of Texas."

The whites were particularly incensed with father over an interview published in the Washington (D. C.) Post, in reference to southern governors attempting to prevent the Sullivan-Kilrain fight, which had been held some months before. Father had said:

"These southern governors are making laughing stocks of themselves by their proclamations. When there are race riots or political outbreaks, they claim to be unable to act unless the sheriffs of the counties where the trouble lies ask for aid; but because a couple of prize-fighters threaten to break the peace by punching each other for a couple of hours, the governors of Louisiana, Mississippi, Arkansas and Texas issued proclamations forbidding the fight and ordering the arrest of the fighters. They did not wait for any appeal from sheriffs, but went ahead.

"Governor Ross of Texas, had beter look at home. Over in Fort Bend County, adjoining Galveston, a lot of young Democratic hot-heads have formed an organization known as 'Jay-birds.' There are about 3000 colored and 200

whites in the County and a mixed ticket is
usually elected with a Democratic sheriff at the
head.   Last Fall there were but two tickets,
the Cleveland and Thurman, which was the conservative ticket, and the 'Jaybirds,' the former
winning.

"The 'Jaybirds' were incensed and disposed
to make trouble. One Gibson, who was the defeated candidate for assessor, tried to pick
a quarrel with Kyle Terry, the successful candidate, and two shots were exchanged in a street
encounter.

"Young Terry is a nephew of Judge Terry of
California, who killed Broderick years ago, and
who recently served six months' imprisonment
for contempt of court. A week or so ago,
Terry was over at Wharton, the county seat of
Wharton County. Gibson was there also, and
had been threatening Terry. The latter, on seeing his enemy approaching, nearly blew Gibson's head off with a double barrelled shot gun.

"It would be a good plan for Governor Ross
to turn his attention to domestic affairs."

CHAPTER XIII.

COLLECTOR OF THE PORT OF GALVESTON.

FOLLOWING the national election, in which the country was carried handsomely by the Republicans, father wrote to Mr. Hackworth at Topeka, Kansas: "I most heartily concur with you in what you say as to the character of some of our Texas Republicans who have held and will attempt to hold again the places of honor and profit in Texas, and think they should not again be trusted with high places. I refer, of course, to those who were so solicitous about the *good name* of Texas when some few of us dared to denounce the outrages of Washington and Fort Bend Counties.

"The Old Party is again in power and I hope it will do what it can to protect its friends in the enjoyment of their political rights in the South, and thereby make it impossible for the oligarchy which has so long ruled the South by murder and fraud, to continue to do so. We shall thereby be enabled to bring this government back to where it shall be ruled by the many and not the few."

After the inauguration of President Harrison, a new era of naval construction was begun, and increasing outlays were made for improvement of rivers and harbors—the latter of direct importance to the deep-water interests of Galveston. A new building for Post Office and Custom House at Galveston was constructed, and father was destined to be the first Collector to occupy it.

There was great pressure brought upon father for patronage in Texas. He found it necessary to reply to one letter, in part: "I do not wish to be harsh in reply to your proposition to pay me for my influence in securing you the position, as you, doubtless, like many others in private life, take it for granted that all public men demand or expect pay from those whom they endorse for public office.

"I simply desire to say it is not a fact. My position in the Republican organization in Texas is of an official nature and as a partisan it is my duty to support those, for official place, of my party faith who are the best fitted to discharge the duties of the offices to which they are appointed, and it was solely upon this ground that I recommended Mr. N—— for appointment."

At Houston, George A. Race was appointed Postmaster in preference to the candidates of the anti-Cuneyites. Of Race's appointment, it was said: "It is an additional evidence that the white leaguers in Texas are getting badly left. The defeat of Strong, Hopkins and Ham, shows that the movement to form an exclusively white man's Republican party was doomed to an early death in Texas."

In July, the new postmaster for Dallas, John S. Witiver, was selected. July 9th saw the appointment, too, of Mrs. Belle Burchill to the Postmastership of the city of Fort Worth. Mrs. Burchill was a good friend of father's and a woman of political sagacity.

When father was asked to throw his influence toward a certain candidate for the Post Office at Abilene, Texas, in opposition to the incumbent, Mrs. Morrow, he replied: "The lady who is Postmaster there is the daughter of a man whose services in behalf of Texas are historical and not only will I refuse to aid anyone to supersede the daughter of General Sam Houston, but I will file a protest with the Department against her removal."

His action met with the commendation of all Texans. The press noted: "The attempt of Col. De Gress to secure the removal of the widowed daughter of Gen. Sam Houston from the Post Office at Abilene has given Cuney another chance to demonstrate his superiority. Cuney's plea for the retention of Mrs. Morrow shows that in spite of his Republicanism, he has the feeling of a Texan and a Texan's pride in the glorious history of his State."

Father's appointment to the position of Collecter of Customs for the port of Galveston was urged by leading business men as well as politicians, and as early as April, he announced his intention of applying for the position. Petitions were also circulated for the appointment of Gen. Malloy.

In opposition to father's candidacy, a Lily White organization, the Central Republican Club of Houston, had a mass meeting and addressed resolutions to the President, which brought forth the following comment from the Houston Post: "The Republican State boss, Mr. Cuney, is not going to retain his position without fighting for it, if there be any virtue in organized opposition. The Republicans are preparing to openly and vigorously wage war on the colored chief, and endeavor to place Republican politics in Texas on a higher plane. Cuney has ridden a very high horse among his Republican brethren. He has been running a kind of Tammany side-show all to himself down here and in the language of this remonstrance, has 'got people scared of him' or words to that effect. These gentlemen who are representing the white wing of the party want to call a halt."

Strange as it may seem, some of the most

serious attempts to "call a halt" to father's appointment, came from Northern Republicans who held that it would be bad policy to appoint a Negro to such an office as the Collectorship of the Galveston port, and that it would have a tendency to irritate the people.

In December, previous, father had been in New York City on business—a visit that was noted by the New York Evening Telegram: "A finely built copper-hued man was being introduced to the leading men about the Fifth Avenue Hotel last night by Col. Thomas Ochiltree; the man was N. Wright Cuney, the leader of the Republican party in Texas and the member of the National Committee from that State."

Later on, in the early summer, another visit to New York, of political importance, was contemplated, and Col. Ochiltree had thought it wise to send the following telegram to the New York Star: "Washington, D. C., May 18—If N. W. Cuney comes to New York, keep mum. Will explain."

How well the injunction was obeyed, this clipping from the Star will show: "Mr. Ochiltree is an ex-Texan member of Congress. Who Cuney is the Star does not know, and why he should come to New York at all, as long as Col. Ochiltree objects, or why the Star should not publish the news in its list of distinguished arrivals, it is still further at a loss to understand. It will promise in advance, however, if Col. Ochiltree's explanation is reasonable not to say another word on the subject. But why this mysterious secrecy? Why should Cuney come to New York if Ochiltree is to be thus incommoded and required to explain? Why is Cuney, anyhow?"

The press was further disturbed: "It has been a severe tax on the brain of the several contributors to this article to decipher what is the real meaning of the mysterious dispatch of Col. Ochiltree to the Star, relative to the importance of not white-washing or otherwise changing the color of Hon. Wright Cuney, the colored candidate for the Collectorship of the port of Galveston. All the facts positively known to be well established which will aid in the deciphering of the dispatch are:

"1. That Prince Ochiltree dispenses the patronage of the State of Texas.

"2. That Wright Cuney is a sagacious Republican politician of Texas, and off color.

"3. That Col. Ochiltree desires that he should be 'kept dark' by the Star which shines for all, even in the dark, and;

"4. That said Cuney wants to be Mr. Blaine's Collector of the port of Galveston, provided there is no Harrison man-relative in the State.

"Do these point to any solution at all? They suggest several guesses,—Did Col. Ochiltree employ the mysterious Cuneyiform cryptographic dispatch mingled with half unintelligible slang to throw the Star off the scent of his purposes —was it his intention to inflict on the good Democratic merchants of Galveston a Republican Collecter of obnoxious hue without their knowledge by asking the only Democratic paper of New York to keep mum as to his dark or darky designs? Or was it the real purpose of Col. Ochiltree to keep the dark gentleman, Cooney or Cuney, as the case may be, in the gloaming, not to say Stygian or Egyptian darkness, while he dispensed the patronage of the port of Galveston through hands that were whiter, though not purer?"

The banter continued: "The mystery deepens as to the precise relations of Ochiltree, the Red Prince Royal of the Lone Star State, and Cuney, or Cooney, the colored candidate for the Custom House at Galveston. From all accounts, Cooney or Cuney has thrown a shadow of gloom around the White House at Washington, in which his chances are obscured; while Prince Ochiltree's advent in the Star office early yesterday afternoon led persons looking west through Park Place into the error of supposing that his red-topped head was the orb of day indulging in an untimely yet golden sunset."

Many replies were sent to the Star,—One

read: "When Frank Hatton captured the Texas colored delegation to the Republican Convention of 1884, for Chester A. Arthur, at a fixed commercial value of $250 a delegate, it was Wright Cuney who lassoed them for Blaine by the cheaper methods of his eloquence. He has been for years past the leader of the Texas Republicans, as Col. Ochiltree has been the dispenser of Texas patronage and of Texas hospitality at the Hoffman House."

Father was invited with the other members of the National Committee to attend the inauguration of General Harrison as President. When father left Galveston for Washington, which was before the New York visit in the summer, he passed through Houston and was met at the depot by a committee of citizens. His presence was immediately noted by a representative of the press: "N. W. Cuney, the noted Texas colored politician, arrived in Houston last night. Of course a Post reporter paid his respects to this stalwart pillar of the Texas Republican party. Mr. Cuney is pleasant in manner and outspoken, and has, more than once in contests with white rivals, demonstrated to an incontrovertible degree, his shrewdness as a politician.

"He leaves on the midnight train—he is going to Washington principally in his own behalf, but also in accordance with an understanding arrived at during the recent Austin conference; that Colonel De Gress has also gone and he, Cuney, would meet him there. 'So far,' he remarked, 'as my going to Washington to dictate appointments or dole out Federal patronage is concerned, that is all gammon. Neither myself nor any other man will be able to do that. General Harrison is not that kind of a man, will not be that kind of President, and you will see that no political bosses, as the term is generally understood, will be tolerated by his administration.'

" 'Good men will be selected to office, the best men to be found, in fact, and each applicant will have to stand on his own merit. I think General Harrison will apply the civil service principle even more rigidly than President Cleveland, and his administration will prove highly patriotic.' "

"To the question: 'What about the appointment of colored men to office?' Cuney replied: 'I don't think there will be any color line any more than a sectional line. I think Mr. Harrison will know no North, South, East or West, and I think he will not inquire about the particular color of a man's skin, so long as he is honest, competent and worthy. The colored people are learning, and many of them are now able to hold office—not only competent, but they have proved themselves worthy.' "

"He was asked: 'What are your chances, do

you think, for the Collectorship at Galveston
and what endorsements do you hold?'

" 'I am backed by the honest people of Galveston,' he said, 'without any regard to party.
All I asked was a testimonial as to my character as an honest, truthful man and upright
citizen, and that I received from the very best
people of Galveston. Those people know me—I
have lived there all my life and they have had
ample opportunity to judge me. I venture to
say that outside of politics you will find none
to condemn me.'

"Mr. Cuney left last night for Washington
via New Orleans. He said he knew of no opposition to himself, but this is a mistake. He will
have very strong opposition. It is going
to be a black versus Lily White fight. The
White Republicans are going to down Cuney if
they can, and if they fail, it will be because of
Mr. Blaine's friendship for the latter."

The Texarkana (Texas) Times said: "We
hope and believe that the merchants and business men of Galveston will at last enter their
protest against the appointment of any Negro
for Collector, even if they fail to recommend a
suitable person. We have made these remarks
because we hear that the business men are paus-
ing as to whether Cuney shall be their choice.
We hope they will not pause longer."

The Star replied to the above: "Unlike the

Times, the Star has no lecture to read to the Galveston business men in advance of any action taken by them on the subject. We believe that as long as their 'blood is thicker than water,' they will do what they believe to be right in the premises."

On the 17th of June, the St. Louis Republic gave a review of the status of the Collectorship case: "Since the withdrawal of De Gress' application for the Collectorship of El Paso, Texas, the Texas patriots have been in a high state of excitement.

"They construe De Gress' action to mean war to the knife. Now that De Gress has no irons of his own in the fire, it is generally expected that he will take occasion to oppose Cuney and in a general way, Cuney's friends. It is believed that Cuney is acting under the advice of Newcomb (?), and it is well known that Newcomb and Cuney have no friendship to waste on each other.

"Newcomb favors a white man's Republican party in Texas, and the exclusion of Negroes from places of power; it is probable that he has coaxed De Gress to fall in with them. . . Russell Harrison is taking a hand in the fight in behalf of Hedges, and so is Chairman Huston of the Indiana State Republican Committee, Mark Hanna and Charley Foster of Ohio, Attorney-General Michener of Indiana and the politicians of influence. R. F. Pancoast of Galveston is also an applicant for the Collectorship. He is an ex-commander of Hancock Post, G. A. R.

"It is thought that Cuney would prefer Pancoast to Hedges, but Cuney will not give up himself until Collector Sweeney's successor is appointed. He will not compromise with anybody or for anything else."

This much is true, for it had been intimated to father that he could have the position of Recorder of Deeds, at Washington, D. C., without opposition, as it had long been a place slated for representative colored politicians. But because of this very fact, and also for the reason that it would take him away from his own State where he felt he could be of greater service to his people, he refused to consider any other position except that of the Collectorship of the Galveston port.

The St. Louis *Republic* declared: "Cuney is insisting on being given the Collectorship at Galveston. He has got a great lot of endorsements from Galveston business men attached to his petition, but there are hints that the administration would prefer a white man for the place. Blaine, who is a man of infinite tact, knows that it would not popularize the administration, to have a Negro in the chief Federal office in Texas, and while friendly to Cuney, he is advising him to seek something else. Cuney, however, is stubborn. He is a 'civil rights' Nigger. He is looking for social recognition and he thinks by being in a position to hold a whip hand over the business men of Galveston—for that matter over a great part of Texas—that he will be able to wipe out, in his case at least, the color line. Besides, Cuney is a business man. Cuney is a boss longshoreman. He employs 300 or 400 men in Galveston and practically has control of the labor on the wharves. But Cuney is not only demanding the Collectorship of the port for himself, he is demanding the appointment of people indorsed by him, for the other Federal offices of the State."

The citizens of Galveston were finally angered at being so severely criticised for desiring father for Collector. The Galveston *Evening Tribune* read: "In a recent issue of the St. Louis *Republic* Mr. O'Brien Moore attempts to draw pen pictures of a few prominent Republicans. Evidently the subjects of his sketches were not present and he drew the portraits from a treacherous and distorted memory. He patronizingly admits that Cuney is a 'smart, industrious fellow.' He says that Cuney is well off. In this he is wrong. Cuney is comparatively a poor man, yet he has never slunk away from a city leaving a long list of unpaid bills—he

has never borrowed money of his friends and
forgotten to repay it—induced them to indorse
him and left them the bag to hold!

"He says that if Blaine becomes a member of
Harrison's cabinet, Cuney will be made Collector
of the port of Galveston, which will be highly
displeasing to the white business men of Galveston, of both parties. It is hardly likely that
Mr. O'Brien Moore has found time in the 'hurly
burly' of 'keeping moving' and drawing 'pen
pictures' to worm his way into the confidence
of Blaine or Harrison, but admitting that his
guesses be correct, why should the business
men of Galveston kick? Mr. Cuney served
the city several times as Alderman, and is now
an honored member of the board of Water Commissioners. If there was no objection to his
making laws for the government of the white
business men of Galveston, why should there
be objection to his collecting Uncle Sam's dues
at this port?"

A Washington special to the Galveston *News*
gave this warning: "If the administration is
really anti-African, it has been suggested that
the failure to give the Galveston Collectorship
to Cuney would be an exceeding explicit way
of showing its hand. As yet nobody believes
that this will happen, for it is claimed that to
turn down Cuney would be disastrous to the
party outside the limits of Texas. It has

reached a point where there is vastly more in it than the fortune of an individual."

Because of the strong opposition aroused solely on account of color, the Collectorship candidacy became one of national interest. It was admitted that no candidate bore higher endorsements than the colored applicant for the position. They were from leading citizens of Galveston and the State at large—business men, bankers, and capitalists—Democrats as well as Republicans.

It was expected by all the members of the National Committee that this appointment would be among those made at least by May. Yet it was constantly delayed at the Treasury Department, although all of the leading officials of the National Committee had seen the President and found him willing to make the appointment.

Time dragged along without action. Friends advised father to remain in Washington until the appointment should be made, but with his active spirit, this was a difficult task. One afternoon in July he went to see his friend Gen. Clarkson at his office in the Post Office Department and told him that he would wait no longer. He asked him to go and see the President with him and get a final answer one way or the other. He was invited by Gen. Clarkson to breakfast with him the next morning, after which they would go to the White House.

Upon their arrival at the White House the following morning they were told that the President was engaged with Mr. Windom, Secretary of the Treasury, signing appointments for that Department. Gen. Clarkson sent in a special request to see the President and was ushered into the office where Secretary Windom and the President were engaged. The appointment that was passed at that particular moment, was for the Collectorship at Galveston, and the President was signing it as Gen. Clarkson entered. He held it out to him and said: "That is right, is it not and as was finally decided upon, isn't it?" Gen. Clarkson replied: "No, Mr. President, that is not the right name. In conferences some of us had with you, with some people from Texas with us, you decided to appoint Mr. Wright Cuney to this place."

The President rose from his chair, and walked over to the window, carrying the appointment with him, and said: "I remember now, but the Department has for some time been advising differently and had caused me to change my mind." Then in an earnest voice he said: "If you were President would you give the most important position in Texas and one of the most important in the whole South, to a Negro?" Gen. Clarkson answered: "Yes, and be glad of the chance, when so worthy and fit a man for the position, and a colored man endorsed as to fitness and reliability for the place by all the Democratic business men of the city, could be found."

The President returned to the table and, scratching out the name he had written, wrote the name of N. Wright Cuney. He then turned to Gen. Clarkson and said: "You are right, and I am glad you called my attention to the matter just in time." Gen. Clarkson went out to father and told him what had happened. He told him to drive with him as far as the Post Office Department and then go to the Capitol where from the gallery he would hear his appointment read. On this day, July 20, 1889, father's nomination as Collector of Customs was sent to the Senate.

Gen. Clarkson has said to me: "I always believed that your father had at times an insight or advance hint into the future, for I saw several instances of it; and I have always believed that he felt, or in some way knew, on the last day he came to me in the Post Office Department, that the next day was to be one of the important days of his whole life, just as it proved to be."

The Washington special to the Galveston News of that date read: "The President did Texas proud to-day by naming three of her

citizens for important places. They were N. W.
Cuney for Collector of Customs at Galveston;
James J. Dickerson of Fort Bend County for
Marshal of eastern district; and Joseph W.
Burke of Austin for Collector of Internal
Revenue for the third Texas district.

"Sweeney, the present Collector at Galveston,
lacked until Oct. 23d next, of completing his
term, so that his is a case of straight removal.
No charges against him were ever talked of
among the Texans here and if any were made
his successor was no party to them.

"Cuney's appointment is not only highly gratifying to his immediate friends, but scores of
people from the States crowded about him when
his success became known, with compliments
and congratulations. Among them several Congressmen and leading politicians. He bears his
honors modestly, yet is evidently full of pride
and happiness at achieving at last the crown-
ing measure of his ambition. It did not take
any peculiar acuteness to see from the start that
he would win. With four such leaders as
Blaine, Allison, Elkins and Clarkson to back
him, how could he fail? Where you have four
aces any novice knows that such a hand is invincible.

"Then too, Cuney played his hand with skill.
He pursued the even tenor of his way and never
lost a jot of his faith in his ultimate victory."

On the first of August, father arrived home from Washington, the successful candidate for "the most important appointment given to a Negro by President Harrison, in point of salary and momentous importance." ,

The Houston Post sarcastically noted: "Down at 'Cuney Island' last night, the elaborate reception prepared for Mr. Cuney, the dark-skinned white man, who was recently given the most important Federal position in Texas by Benjamin Harrison, took place."

There were comments, favorable and otherwise. From far distant Iowa, appeared an editorial in the Iowa Register: "One of the most satisfactory and most gratifying appointments so far, is that of Mr. N. W. Cuney, to be Collector of Customs at Galveston. He has been the Texas member of the Republican National Committee for several years, and has been unusually efficient and valuable to the party in that position. He is a man of bright mind, quick understanding, good judgment and a large endowment of common sense, united with a character whose integrity has never been challenged.

"He will make a very efficient officer and will discharge the duties of his position in a manner acceptable alike to the Government and to the business interests of Galveston.

"The selection for this important place, of

a man who has done a great deal of hard work for the party, will greatly please the Republicans of Texas, and is a fitting recognition of a good and true man."

The *Post,* of Houston, gave its parting shot: "If any single consideration outside of partisan politics entered into Cuney's appointment, it was the remarkable endorsement which the business men of Galveston, depending upon Democratic patronage and trade, furnished. So between the rank partisanship of the administration, backed and solicited by the Galveston merchants, it happens that one of the most offensive Republican Negro politicians and bosses of Texas, is fastened upon the business of the State for the next four years, as Collector of the port of Galveston."

The Galveston *News* gave a terse rejoinder: "Its animus is too perspicuous to deceive any of the friends of Democratic Galveston."

The Indianapolis (Ind.) World thought: "The appointment of Mr. Cuney is the best that the President has made—in view of his unselfish devotion and sacrifice in behalf of his people. Mr. Cuney has for years been an unselfish worker in the Republican ranks, and for honor, probity and moral worth, no man stands higher."

The St. Louis Republic continued: "Cuney was backed by nearly every prominent Republican and politician in Texas and had the solid support of the members of the Republican National Committee. He was also endorsed by a number of prominent merchants in Galveston, Democrats as well as Republicans. It was these endorsements from Galveston that secured the office for Cuney.

"The President in announcing his Southern policy in the early days of his administration, said that he would not appoint any Negroes to local offices where such appointment would be offensive to white men.

"It is understood that in discussing with himself and others, over the appointment of Cuney, he excused himself on the ground that Cuney's appointment could not be offensive to the white people of Galveston and Texas because a number of them asked for his appointment."

The San Antonio *Light,* one of the few leading Republican papers of the State, published an open letter: "It must be a source of particular gratification to Mr. Cuney, that no one has seen fit, or is able to deny his peculiar fitness for this office, to which he has been appointed, though unsparing in their criticisms.

"His ability is unquestioned and as long as this remains to his credit, he has nothing to fear. Mr. Cuney enjoys the confidence of his race in a far greater degree than many of the so-called leaders. A determination to remain loyal to them at all hazards, has characterized his every action, and it is this which has won for him the reputation which he enjoys to-day. A better selection could not have been made. It is not the purpose of this article to indulge in any particular eulogy of the Negro, but it does seem that when an important position is given a Negro, a few disgruntled politicians should cease nursing their sore thumbs and come out on the side of justice."

When Gov. Coke of Texas was asked if he would oppose father's confirmation as Collector, he replied: "No, Sir, Cuney is President Harrison's appointee and on him rests the responsibility for the appointment. There is no objection to Cuney, save his color."

When the appointment came before the Senate, Senator Coke remained neutral, while Senator Reagan of Texas voted to confirm him. In January, 1890, father relieved Capt. C. C. Sweeney. Dr. George M. Patten, the son of Nathan Patten, a former Collector of Customs, was selected as his Deputy, and the personnel of the office made up of efficient men, about equally divided among white and colored.

CHAPTER XIV.

The Color Bar.

Outside of politics, the years 1890 and 1891 were uneventful. Father was active in the State. At the request of the people he visited many of the County fairs, delivered addresses on the tariff, industrial conditions, education, the Negro question and other live issues of the day.

At the founding of Langston City, Oklahoma, father wrote to the Hon. E. P. McCabe: "I believe you are on the right course; such an enterprise will, I hope, prove beyond question that the race is capable of uniting and doing that which cannot fail to elicit favorable commendation."

Other enterprises of the people of color in the South were now being considered. The colored institutions of learning were rapidly growing in Texas, and father, alive to their needs, was constantly in demand—giving advice and working for their cause.

As a mark of recognition of his interest in general education, public schools were being given his name.

To the principal of the N. W. Cuney School at Whitesborough, Texas, he wrote: "Please convey to the trustees, patrons and pupils, my high appreciation of the mark of confidence and respect shown by them in the naming of their school for me.

"Say to the little ones for me, that they cannot realize, at the present time, the significance of their action and my appreciation thereof.

"It is truly gratifying that the youth in our public schools should appreciate me for doing those things in my public life which I believe to be right and for the best interests of our common country.

"None of the living can now say but what some of the little ones in that group, actuated by an ambition to serve their fellow man and the interests of our country, may yet be called upon to fill the highest positions in the gift of the people. But in this they should remember that integrity and intelligence and patience are the essential qualities in life, for success.

"I send herewith a flag, the emblem of our country. May you impress upon their minds, young as they are, the significance of this emblem to themselves and their posterity—teach them to cherish it, to love it and if necessary to die for it."

As early as 1889, a separate coach bill was

proposed and father wrote to Representatives
George W. Bryan and Walter Gresham of the
Texas State Legislature:

"Some one has sent me a copy of S. B. No. 18,
offered by Mr. Pope, proposing to require the
railroads to furnish separate cars for white and
colored passengers. I see by the papers that the
bill has reached the House and been referred to
the proper committee.

"I am grieved to see the Legislature falling
into the error of legislating on this subject
which is clearly not within its province. Besides, all such legislation is futile and iniquitous
and cannot possibly withstand our advancing
humanity and civilization. Such a law would be
a disgrace to the State, in the eyes of enlightened
mankind, and a severe reflection upon the wisdom of a people, whose Representatives attempted to preserve in law a prejudice
which the growing humanity and intelligence
of the people they misrepresented in the matter
had more than half overcome. The fact that
the Senate passed the bill is no sufficient evidence that the people are crying for this species
of legislation. Had a large number of the
Legislature come to Austin demanding legislation of the kind, one might say that there was
considerable demand for it; but there is nothing
of the kind and I think the Senate has care-
lessly and out of complaisance to one of its mem-

bers permitted him to use it to gratify his ambition for injuring the weak and unoffending.

"I think it an undeniable fact that if there was any great public demand for separate cars in this State, the Railroad would put them on in obedience to the demand and I can assure you that it would be far more desirable to be wronged by a Railroad Corporation than by the State, which I ought to and want to love.

"Hundreds, perhaps, of white and colored people transact business on the cars going from place to place, but under this bill they will be denied this privilege. Look at the bill in any light you may, one is forced to the conclusion that it is uncalled for, unwise, a violation of the rights of property, and a brutal invasion of the rights of a people whose consciences will feel keenly the wrong done them by the 'New South' in its effort to reverse fate and check the growth of a broader and better humanity.

"Protestation may be useless where folly holds the reins but I protest against this outrageous injustice."

During the year 1891, the separate coach law was enacted by the Twenty-second Legislature of Texas—the first in the State, of a series of unjust and pernicious legislation.

On Sept. 11, 1891, the colored men of the State, irrespective of political affiliation, held a successful convention at Galvestion. Committees were formed on Emigration, World's Fair and Education. Opposition was made to a separate department for colored exhibits at the World's Fair, and a special address issued to the Governor and the people of the State, against the separate coach bill. Rev. I. B. Scott, now Bishop of the Methodist Episcopal Church, was, with my father, commended as one of the Commissioners at the World's Fair at Chicago.

About this time, my parents decided that I should attend the New England Conservatory of Music at Boston, Mass., where I might complete my general education, and at the same time have the advantage of a thorough musical training. After a summer spent in Newport, R. I., my mother made arrangements for my entering the Institution. One other colored student, besides myself, occupied a room in the Conservatory home, and for a short while there was no unpleasantness on account of color.

Nevertheless, late in October, my father received a letter from the executive committee saying:

"Your daughter, with other colored pupils who have entered the Home of the Institution, was received in good faith and has enjoyed its every privilege; but we find ourselves confronted with a problem growing out of their connection with the Home, which seriously affects the interests of the Conservatory—a problem for which there seems no adequate solution save in the disposition of the parents of colored pupils to provide them homes outside the Conservatory. We have a large number of pupils who are affected by race prejudices, and the Home must be conducted so as to insure the comfort and satisfaction of the largest number possible, otherwise its success, and the success of the Institution, which is entirely dependent upon its patronage, is imperilled.

"Further, despite our best effort, we realize that we cannot save the colored ladies in the Home, from the possibility of disagreeable experiences, and while all the educational advantages of the Institution are open to them, it seems advisable for their own comfort, for the stability and welfare of the Institution whose advantages they covet and enjoy, and for the advantage of all concerned, that they make their home with friends outside."

My father replied: "I notice with extreme reluctance the bewildering fact that glorious Massachusetts, with her long line of immortal heroes—William L. Garrison, Wendell Phillips, Chas. Sumner, John A. Andrews, John Boyle O'Reilly, and a whole host of noble men and women too numerous to mention, can furnish an institution of learning, capable of surrendering her world-wide fame, won in the fields of humanity and christian endeavor, at

Maud Cuney Hare

the demand of a dying prejudice which your great State has done so much towards rendering nauseous in the eyes of enlightened humanity.

"Publications and catalogues attracted my attention to your institution. I accepted your invitation to the world to embrace its advantages for my child. I believed that your principles were fixed in the foundations of humanity, justice and honor, and not subject to the control of a few misguided girls or parents.

"I thought you had counted all the trifling costs and were braced for them. Judge, then, how greatly I have been deceived by your attitude in printed solicitations for patronage.

"You request my co-operation in surrendering to the demands of prejudice, by withdrawing my daughter; I cannot help you. Ask Massachusetts; ask her mighty dead; ask her living sons and daughters. They will co-operate with you, if you cannot solve the problem, and render your Institution illustrious throughout all ages."

To me he wrote at the same time:

"You were quite right, darling, when you said that you knew your father would tell you to stay. I can safely trust my good name in your hands. I wish you were where I could embrace and kiss you but will have to content myself with kissing your photo on my desk which I now do.

Your conduct, dear, in this case meets my entire approval and makes me doubly proud of you. I only hope to see you pull through in your studies. I know you will make no mistakes as to your conduct in school, knowing so well who you are. Why did you not answer my telegram? All of our friends here admire your pluck. I have been very busy in public matters. They are now out of the way and I shall only live now for mama, you and Lloyd. I am still troubled with insomnia but hope to get over the trouble soon. I was preparing to sue the Institution if they dared force you out of the building."

I refused to leave the dormitory, and because of this, was subjected to many petty indignities. I insisted upon proper treatment. The attitude of myself and my parents was displeasing to the Conservatory management, but the instructors were just and the matter was finally adjusted by my remaining in the 'Home.'

The directors later publicly declared that the whole matter arose from a "misunderstanding" and that there was no color bar in the institution.

CHAPTER XV.

POLITICS AGAIN.

FATHER'S attention was again turned to political matters. In January, 1891, regarding the candidacy of Mr. Ingalls of Kansas for the U. S. Senatorship, father wrote Judge S. Hackworth of Topeka:

"It is not necessary for me to remind you of the fact that Louisiana, South Carolina, old Virginia, Alabama, Florida, Georgia and Arkansas are dominated to-day by an oligarchy just as relentless as it was before the late war. We in Texas, outside of a few counties, are relieved of that, but you know the reason why.

"Remember that Kansas was first made known by the heroic deeds, in the struggle for human liberty, of the lamented John Brown and Jim Lane, and for more than a decade the eloquent tongue and the magic genius of John J. Ingalls have kept her before the public as the home of a people who have done so much for human freedom and enlightened progress. If such a man is to be defeated by such a people it gives little encouragement, to those of us who live in the far distant South, to continue the struggle for those principles which he and they have so continuously, nobly and ably defended.

"I can not believe that the people of Kansas, who have made their State the home of the oppressed for these many years will, at this late day so far forget the noble deeds of their ancestors, as to take such a step backward, and defeat the election of Mr. Ingalls, and thus give strength to that element referred to, which rules the South with a mailed hand. I believe all true Republicans in the South and lovers of human liberty everywhere view with alarm the possible defeat of Mr. Ingalls, the silver-tongued pleader for a free ballot, a fair count and the rights of humanity. Kansas, in my judgment, in the defeat of Mr. Ingalls, will lose that proud position which she occupies in the eyes of enlightened civilization acquired by his genius and eloquence. I know there is a great unrest among the producing classes of our country, but I cannot see how in view of the fact that the South is solid and ruled by an oligarchy, the defeat of Mr. Ingalls will better their condition. In short, can Kansas take this step twenty-five years backward and extend aid to the same men who struggled so hard to overthrow those principles which she so nobly defended? I notice the Democratic press now proposes to use the defeat of Senator Wade Hampton as a reason why Senator Ingalls should be defeated. Mr. Irby promises to carry out the policy defended by Mr. Hampton. Our friends in Kansas should observe that the alliance in the South do not advance on the principles of the Democratic party because they are Democrats, yet they ask and urge the Republicans of the North and West to forsake all that has made them so great and break away from the principles of that party which they fought and died to sustain. I, in the name of the Republicans of the South, hope their chalice will pass from our lips and that they will stand firmly by those principles, so ably defended by Garrison, Phillips, Butler, Sumner and a host of those who have made our country as glorious as it is. With the best of wishes for the success of Mr. Ingalls, I am yours very truly,

N. W. CUNEY."

In Texas politics, following the usual county and congressional conventions, the State convention was held on Sept. 4th in San Antonio. There the "Lily Whites," who were constantly engaged in improving their plans to free themselves from contact with the colored voter, were again defeated.

In an interval which followed, father had occasion to reply to a correspondent, relative to political questions before the people. He said, in part: "I have, since my return home, read

your letter very carefully and have arrived at
the conclusion that your proposition is not a
practical one, but the earnestness in which you
write and the undoubted sincerity which shows
upon the face of your letter demand at my hand
reasons for this conclusion.

"In the first place, this is a political question
in which all people should be free to act according to their judgment as to what is for the best
interests of our State. If the question is detri-
mental to the laboring interests of our State,
then, in my judgment, all the laboring interests without reference to nationality should take
action against it.

"In the second place: If there is any one
thing in our public relations I abhor and detest
it is the question of the injustice therein of
color, religion or nationality, and it has been
the labor of my public life for twenty years,
to eliminate these elements from our public
policy.

"The Negro is a part of the citizenship of our
country, endowed with all the rights under the
constitution which are enjoyed by any other
class of citizens, and equally responsible for
the good or evil which may flow from the performance of his public duties, and in my opinion it is the duty of all right-thinking men
continually to impress this upon his mind,
thereby making the citizenship of our common

country thoroughly homogeneous in all of its public relations.

"Whatever concerns the Negro for weal or woe of our country must necessarily concern all. While I thoroughly concur with you that under the prevailing circumstances the commission amendment should not be adopted, yet I feel, as a citizen, that we should act in casting our votes, solely as citizens without reference to color.

"In the third place: I note what you say about secret societies working in this matter. My opinion is that if secret societies attempt to shape the public policy of our country, they then become dangerous and inimical to the public welfare and democratic institutions. In this lies the danger of the growth of secret societies among the thoughtless in our country, and in my judgment it behooves all patriotic citizens to keep them as far removed from public matters as possible and to impress continually upon their leaders that their duties are benevolent and not political, as they would create factions which would be injurious to the public good."

In the Fall of 1891, a pleasant incident was the welcoming in port of the new revenue cutter Galveston. Oct. 21, Mayor Fulton and Secretary Dana of the Chamber of Commerce appointed a reception committee, for the purpose of going aboard the cutter and extending the formal welcome. At the appointed time, Mayor

Fulton, P. J. Willis, J. M. Lee, W. F. Turnley,
Secretary Dana, L. S. McKinney, H. Austin,
R. M. Cash, and father, with the members of the
artillery company were on hand. Mayor Fulton,
Mr. Dana and father delivered the addresses
of welcome, which were happily responded to
by Capt. Munger.

On Nov. 24th the National Republican Committee met in Washington, D. C., where there
was a most spirited contest for the National
Convention. Father was especially honored in
the meeting of the Committee, by being called
by Gen. Clarkson, to preside. Ex-Governor
Pinchback of Louisiana had opportunity during the afternoon recess, to denounce the white
Republicans of the South, whom he said, he
"held to be responsible for the lack of virility
of the party in that section of the country, and
for suppressing the Negro vote for fear of race
issues." At the night session, the intrepid
Governor Foraker of Ohio spoke, and was received with the greatest enthusiasm. It was
reported that: "His friends he pleased, by his
magnificent speech; his enemies he disappointed,
because they could find nothing to criticise.
Many of them he won over to himself and
made them his lasting friends. There was not
a man in that great crowd who did not admire
Gov. Foraker after he had finished his speech.
There was not one who did not acknowledge

his greatness and applaud him to the echo. Many did not know him, and when they saw the kind of man he is, they were not surprised that Ohio loves him." Governor-elect McKinley of Ohio, was also one of the speakers at the meeting.

After the claims of each city for the National Convention had been heard, Minneapolis, Minn., was decided upon, and the time, the 7th of June, 1892.

Upon father's return from Washington, he was interviewed by a representative of the Galveston *News.* To the first question, as to whether Blaine and Clarkson would oppose Harrison, he replied: "Mr. Blaine is a statesman, he believes in protection and reciprocity measures, not men, and no one can question his fidelity to these principles.

"I know Mr. Clarkson well. The fact of his having accepted a position on the executive committee without reference to what may have been his position before the convention, is evidence that he is enlisted for the war, and those who know the manly heart and loyal Republicanism of Mr. Clarkson will never believe him capable of engaging in what is commonly known in politics as 'knifing.' Our Democratic friends will learn this by the Ides of November."

As to the policy of the Senate relative to silver, father replied: "The policy of the Re-

publican party as evidenced by its stand in the
last Congress is in direct opposition to the free
coinage of silver.

"It is also well known that eight Republican
senators representing the silver producing
States, voted in favor of free coinage, and I
take it for granted, as Mr. Stewart has rein-
troduced his bill favoring free coinage, it is
an open question whether these gentlemen will
relinquish their former stand upon this subject.
We have had two acquisitions to the Senate,
Mr. Hill from New York and Mr. Brice from
Ohio. Both gentlemen, it is supposed, represent
the eastern idea on the silver question. This
in all probability will somewhat complicate the
situation and render it nearly impossible for any
one to give an accurate idea of the situation.

"The Cleveland, Mills, Morrison and Carlisle faction desired to force the issue between
the two great parties on the tariff question
solely and avoid the silver question.

"On the other hand Hill, Gorman and Tammany were favorable to a marked neutrality
in the party's attitude on these questions.''

The Galveston Custom House

CHAPTER XVI.

FIGHTING THE "LILY WHITES."

In the Spring of 1892, following the County Convention at Beaumont, at which the Cuneyites had been victorious, Henry G. Baxter, chairman of the Jefferson County Republican Executive Committee, addressed an open letter to father. Calling attention to the statistics concerning the Negro population and illiteracy, the communication stated:

"There are some few exceptions, I will admit, men like you and Fred Douglass, who have the intelligence and ability to understand and analyze the great principles of political economy underlying the Republican platform.

"But such men as you among the Negro race are few, and may I ask if you can be classed as a pure-blooded Negro? Is there not some potent, unacknowledged factor which raises you and Fred Douglass in intelligence and ability, over the average Negro of pure African descent?

"There is a dangerous spirit fostering among the Negroes, a desire to control the party actions, in which they happen to be, in point of numbers, the most numerous of the Republicans. Can

they, to the exclusion of the white Republicans,
or 'Lily Whites,' as the most virulent Negroes
call the earnest white Republican standard-
bearers, afford to form a distinctly Negro party?
Will the whites who have so long been dominant
by birth, education, numbers and social dis-
tinctions, submit to Negro domination?

"Are the Negroes prepared to prove that they
are morally, intellectually and physically prepared to control the reins of government should
they be able to seize hold of them?"

This sentiment was not unknown in the North.
In the preceding campaign in Michigan, the
chairman of the Republican Committee of that
State declared that the party had done enough
for the Negroes and called them insolent for
requesting recognition.

It was evident that the Republican party in
the South, with the exception, of course, of a few
fair-minded members of the white race, meant to
be free, at all hazards, "from the Negro as a
race."

There were no serious objections to the few
who "knew their place," but the party control
must be in the hands of the white man and he
was fast perfecting organization to that end.
The colored men were just as determined to prevent this injustice, which could only lead to
general disfranchisement.

Father declared, "The 'Lily White' movement

is incoherent, having no principle to back it, and it is based entirely on racial prejudices. It must therefore pass away, leaving no signs of its present existence save a sulphurous name."

On March 9th, the Republican State convention met at Austin, to select delegates to the National Convention. This convention was one of the largest attempted for years. It was prophesied—"Cuney will undoubtedly attempt to control the convention, but he will have trouble—it is evident that the 'Lily White' movement will control the coming meetings."

Mr. Charles Ferguson, who was an anti-administration man, had allied himself with the opposition, and was supported by the "Lily Whites."

In the temporary organization, the Committee on Credentials held a long and stormy session. Delegates who held prima facie credentials were to be admitted in the temporary organization, but the concluding phrase of Chairman Lock McDaniel's call, issued three weeks before the convention, was the proviso: "With the exception of those cases where contestants, within five days of the meeting of said convention, have filed their contests with the chairman of the State Executive Committee, with printed grounds of contest." This ruling practically barred out all delegations wherein contests occurred, and in every case the "Lily Whites" had contested the Cuney delegations.

Father, claiming it was simply a scheme to legislate in favor of the "Lily Whites," assailed this rule, and made a motion to seat those contesting delegates who held prima facie credentials—a law that had been followed in previous conventions.—"One man attempts to dictate to this committee," he said. "What are we here for? There are thirty-one men to transact the business of the party. There are enough honest men in the committee to do what is right, and to the gentleman who presides, I say we have no master in this country, and as far as Wright Cuney is concerned, no slaves." His motion was almost unanimously carried.

The Galveston-Dallas *News* reported: "The news was rushed to the impatient delegates in the Convention hall and the colored men roared their approval. . . . But for the splendid leadership of Cuney and the thorough discipline of his following, the 'Lily Whites' would have made a better fight."

"On the second day there was much excitement attending the seating of contesting delegations. The motion of Charles Ferguson to unseat the Fort Bend delegation was defeated by a vote of 483 to 145. A bystander remarked: 'The truth appears to be that the "Lily Whites" have more voices than votes.' "

Before the election of the delegates-at-large,
Hon. Lock McDaniel, chairman of the State
Executive Committee, said: "There is no one
opposed to Cuney's being elected a delegate-
at-large to the National Convention. The trouble
is that Ferguson wants to go to the National
Convention with a number of delegates in favor
of him so as to supplant Cuney and have himself
elected as member of the National Committee.
There are to be eight delegates-at-large elected
to the National Convention, and two from each
of the eleven congressional districts. These
thirty delegates elect the member of the National
Executive Committee, and it is this position
which Ferguson is after. Mr. Cuney will win,
but if he does not you can put it down that no
colored man will be elected in his stead."

In father's speech before the convention, he
alluded to the unnecessary strife which had been
engendered in the party in the State. He said
that he had been forced into a contest of no seeking of his own—in a strife which had assumed
a personal attitude toward him on the question
of "Cuney or no Cuney." This was largely, he
contended, on account of the opposition to him
from the Democratic press on the assumption
that he was leader of the Republicans. "I
assume," he said, "no such leadership. There are
too many far abler men than I in the party.
Nor have I ever attempted to dictate as to

what should be the policy of our party in Texas.

"Still I will not stand idle and indifferent and see its principles prostituted for selfish purposes. I have not schemed to tie up delegations in order to rob the people of any honest expression of their opinions and political wishes. I feel that I can confidently leave everything to the convention and trust to its fairness in all matters of interest to the success of our party.

"We had a fair solution of such difficulties in our temporary organization yesterday and in the election of our distinguished and fair-minded chairman, Hon. J. B. Rector.

"I am before you as a candidate, but even in that it is not of my own seeking. I have been forced into it as a matter of personal pride.

"When cliques determine that, by the eternal gods, Cuney shall not go to the convention, then I say it is time for the people to act upon some higher motive then 'downing Cuney.' As to the complaint that white men have been prevented from voting for the Republican ticket because President Harrison honored me with the appointment of Collector of the port of Galveston, I do not believe it. If it is true, such men had better vote the Democratic ticket."

Judge Rosenthal, chairman of the committee read the report of the committee on Credentials, and after considerable discussion, it was adopted.

All of the Cuney delegates were seated. Every opposing measure advanced by the "Lily Whites" was vetoed, while the differences with the Ferguson faction were compromisd. The Cuneyites were jubilant.

At an early hour, March tenth, the convention completed the election of its eight delegates-at-large to the National Convention at Minneapolis, who were instructed to vote for Benjamin Harrison. The delegation stood: John B. Rector, W. F. Crawford, Lock McDaniel, A. J. Rosenthal, A. Asbury, Fred Chase, C. M. Ferguson and N. W. Cuney. The four first named were white and the others, colored delegates. The Cuneyites had elected seven out of the eight delegates-at-large.

There was long cheering and cries for the "Yellow Rose of Texas." Father responded heartily, thanking the convention for the largest majority vote which was cast by it, for him.

The "Lily White" leaders took a back seat and some of them left the hall, swearing that they would no longer affiliate with the party. A long struggle had been made to get control of the regular Republican party organization in Texas, but they were at last forced to give up the fight.

On March 10th, after the adjournment of the regular convention, James P. Newcomb, leader of the "Lily White" faction, called a mass con-

vention of his followers to meet in Dallas on
April 12th, for the purpose of nominating a
State ticket and of selecting delegates to the
National Convention, in opposition to the dele-
gates just selected by the regular organization.

After bolting, Col. Newcomb declared there
was "much dissension in the colored ranks on
account of Cuney not being able to provide all
of his 'black cohorts' with a position at the
Custom House—the Negro will act the Trojan
horse and help bring about the plan of keeping
the Negro in the rear."

The "Lily White" convention, pursuant to Col.
Newcomb's call, was held in Dallas, April 12,
1892. It was the first white Republican convention ever held in the State of Texas.

In a lengthy address to the convention, Judge
Henry Cline of Houston said in part: "Do you
not feel the strong current of your Gothic blood
stir in your veins to-day? Are you ready to
assert the spirit of white men in this country and
govern it? To do this we have to get rid of
Negro domination. My God! when I think of
the Austin Convention! A colored man, sitting
at the receipt of Customs in Galveston, a tax
collector, told us if we did not like the way the
Republican party was managed we could vote
the Democratic ticket." He advised that the
Negroes who wished to be Republicans should
work separately from the whites.

Colonel Kindred of Amarillo proposed to re-nominate and re-elect the good men that were elected by the Austin Convention, because some of them he declared, (presumably the whites) were true and representative men. The "white" convention chose delegates to the National Convention and nominated a complete State ticket, naming Col. A. J. Houston of Dallas, the son of the illustrious Sam Houston, for Governor, with Col. Newcomb for Lieutenant-Governor.

In Col. Houston's address, which was decidedly conservative, he said: "You must all know that I have not sought this. There are other men far more competent and I opposed nominations at this time, not for any particular reasons, but because the combined wisdom of conservative men opposed it for reasons seemingly good."

In the address to the Republicans of the State, the "white" convention appealed to the people for consideration for "the new departure we have taken as a representative body of white Republicans of Texas. We feel justified in assuming that the Republican party has no organization such as is recognized as requisite to constitute a political party—therefore the necessity has arisen for the organization of the Republican party of Texas, independent of its past history, and upon the further recognition of the fact that only upon the intelligence and manhood of the white American citizen, can any party in this country hope for growth and success.

"We call upon the white Republicans of the State, and those in sympathy with the principles and policies of the Republican party, to come to our aid and give us their assistance in building up Republicanism in Texas. We call upon the white Republicans of the State to organize and come to the support of our standard bearers in the coming State election."

The New York Herald, in making a survey of the national situation in May, received among their replies, the two following despatches: "Galveston, May 28, 1892. The Texas delegation is practically unanimous for Harrison. Opposed to free coinage and in favor of the McKinley bill. N. W. Cuney."

"Paris, Texas, May 28, 1892. The white Republicans of Texas are now thoroughly organized and will favor the most valuable man for President. We object to Texas federal patronage being dispensed by Negroes. We favor limited coinage of silver and protective tariff. S. J. Wright."

At the Republican National Convention which was held on June 7th at Minneapolis, the delegates selected by the White Republican convention appealed their case to the highest tribunal of the party—the Committee on Credentials of the National organization. They demanded recognition as the duly accredited delegates of the Republican party of Texas.

The National Convention in adopting the report of its Committee on Credentials decided that the "Lily Whites" were "not only not entitled to seats in the convention, but represented a political organization in Texas which is un-American and un-Republican." The defeat of the "Lily Whites" was complete. Father was re-appointed National Committeeman for the State of Texas.

In the National Convention there were one hundred and twenty colored delegates, among them Hon. Frederick Douglass, who favored the re-nomination of Pres. Harrison. Out of the thirty Texas delegates, father held twenty-two solid for Harrison. At the close of the convention, Senator Quay remarked to father: "You are responsible for Harrison's nomination."

From Minneapolis, father went to Washington, and then, early in July, came to New York to join me that we might have the journey home together.

While we were staying at the Hotel St. Nicholas an amusing incident occurred. One morning, having retired late the previous evening, breakfast hour was nearly past before we were ready to enter the dining-room. Father suggested that I precede him and order breakfast. The cashier noticed my sitting alone, and coming to the table she began the conversation by asking if I was waiting for my husband. To my laughing exclamation that it was my father whom I was with, she said: "Oh, Spanish girls marry when so very young, we in the hotel thought that you were a little Spanish girl-bride." When I declared my race, she cried in astonishment: "But you and your father must be Spanish! No? Then Creole—surely you can not be colored."

Then continued an expression of bewildered, hazy ideas concerning the results of race admixture—texture of hair and shade of complexion, which led to a serious discussion of the Negro problem.

When father came to the table, I told him of the incident. He said; "You did right in declaring your race." He abhorred above all things the supposedly easier way of "passing for white," and instilled in my young brother and me a hatred and contempt for the cowardly method which is upheld by many who can successfully disown their Negro blood.

July ninth saw us en route to Galveston via the steamship Concho of the Mallory Line. Captain Risk, who was a good friend of father's, did all in his power to make our voyage a most delightful one.

A passenger of interest, Edwin Markham, said among other things in his "Sketch made at Sea" for the New York Mail and Express: "Judge

Story said, 'We stand the latest, and if we fail, probably the last experiment of self-government by the people. Hon. Wright Cuney, the head of the Republican party in Texas and Collector of the Port of Galveston, is one of the men to make the experiment successful. He is among our passengers, returning with his daughter to their home and his post."

Shortly after father's return home, the Republican State Convention was held. This convention, which met September 12th at Fort Worth, had two objects in view—the consideration and endorsement of the National platform and to consult the best interests of Texas in the matter of State officials.

Many important elections had been lost in 1891, the country was Democratic, and there was no ray of hope for the election of a Republican governor in Texas.

Realizing the conditions, the leading Republicans, Hawley, Rosenthal, Hunt, McCormick, Webster Flanagan, father and others opposed the nomination of a State ticket. They believed it for the best interests of the State to endorse one of the candidates already in the field.

The regular Democratic party of the State had nominated Gov. Hogg for re-election, while the progressive element had bolted and selected Judge Clark. The two other candidates, exclusive of Col. A. J. Houston of the "Lily

Whites," were Thomas L. Nugent, Populist, and
D. M. Prentice, Prohibitionist.

In spite of the split with the "Lily Whites,"
the majority of the delegates were white, and the
attendance unusually large. After minor difficulties, temporary organization was completed
by the election of Hon. R. B. Hawley of Galveston for chairman, and H. M. Tarver of Brenham,
a young colored delegate, for Secretary.

"Save the State" was the sentiment of the convention. The majority declared that this could
be best effected by endorsing Judge Clark, while
the remaining delegates were divided between
those who favored a Republican State ticket
and those who wished to "Turn Texas loose"
by instructing for no particular candidate.

Concerning the proceedings of the last day of
the convention, the Galveston *News* reported:
"Cuney saved the day by quiet work and a well-
timed speech. The people who were against
Clark sent their people to the front and kept
up a continuous cheering. Arch Cochran made
a flash movement and things had a squally look
judging from appearances. Behind the chairman sat Cuney. He waited until the anti-
endorsers had spent their eloquence. When
the other side had exhausted its eloquence, a
long, lean colored delegate got up on a chair and
yelled, 'Cuney.' Delegate after delegate who
had been sitting as still as a wooden Indian while

the opposition cheered, waked into life and called for the Galveston man.

"The speech moved the convention. His scathing excoriation of Hoggism and third partyism (Lily White), recalled the convention from its dream of being free. His unyielding advocacy of Judge Clark as the only man the Republicans could vote for in Texas, blazed the way. The others followed. The Clark people had their forces well in hand. Governor Hogg had lieutenants on the ground. Webster Flanagan told a *News* reporter that he was approached by one.

"Rumor said Cluney had been approached by another, but when asked about it, Cuney laughed and held his peace."

After the debate on the question, the vote was taken and the result of the balloting was an endorsement of Judge Clark. When the vote was announced, the hall was shaken with tremendous cheering, and the recommendation made unanimous.

Because of the criticism occasioned by his advocacy of Judge Clark, father published the following explanatory letter:

"In view of the result of the recent Fort Worth Convention, in which I had the honor to play an active part, I have been called upon by many friends, who were not present, to explain my reasons for advocating such action.

"Under ordinary circumstances I would have

favored a straight Republican ticket, for every
one knows I am a Republican and wish to uphold
Republican principles, but experience has taught
me that we could not accomplish anything for
Texas or our party by putting a ticket in the
field. We have an undisputed power as a bal-
lance but absolutely no power as a prime factor.
The largest vote we, as a party, ever polled in
Texas for Governor was in 1890, when we gave
Gen. Flanagan 77,000 votes.

"I knew under existing circumstances, that
Mr. Hogg, Mr. Clark or Mr. Nugent would be
the next Governor of Texas.

"Realizing that it was a state matter, and in no
way connected with National politics, and realizing that every citizen of Texas owes his State
a great and solemn obligation, I could not see
wherein I was untrue to the National party,
to which I belong, in advocating the recommendation of Judge Clark, as I thought best,
to the support of the Republicans of Texas.

"I examined the principles advocated by each
of these gentlemen, as to the best political and
material interest of the State, and when I say
that, of course, I mean the best interest of each
individual in his daily life. I considered the
condition of every home and fireside—its prosperity and happiness. I lost sight of personal
preferences and personal prejudices.

"It is almost useless, at this time, to go into

details and state specific reasons, as I shall later on do so before the people of Texas when I meet them.

"Mr. Hogg has been our Governor for two years and what has been the result? Stagnation in business, no new enterprises, every industry paralyzed, money driven from the State, the money market in the hands of a few at the expense of the many—this to such an extent that the rate of interest has gone up to 10 and 12 per cent., so that Texas to-day is doing business at pawn shop rates. Many if not most farmers are borrowers, and it is strange to me that they and their fellow citizens, who are thinking people, cannot or do not see the injuries inflicted upon them by the reckless class of legislation adopted by the present administration, all of which goes to prove the total incapacity of the administration to conduct the government in the interest of the whole people.

"I objected to Mr. Nugent because he is in line with Mr. Hogg; but a few steps removed toward socialism and communism—for instance, the Government ownership of railroads and the subtreasury. His principles seek to undermine our whole system of business, which has existed for years, and under which our country has become great and strong, and made itself the foremost among the nations of the world.

"It was therefore clear to me for the foregoing

reasons and others too plain to mention that the
best thing for the Republicans to do at this junc-
ture, important to all the vital interests of the
State, was to refrain from putting a State ticket
in the field and lend a helping hand to that
element most likely to remove the disastrous
effect of the Hogg Hurricane, universally admitted to be the worst which has ever swept over
Texas.

"The Convention has now passed into history
and the atmosphere has cleared, and looking
dispassionately at its work I am more than ever
fully convinced that it has done a wise, sagacious and patriotic piece of work which will
redound to its credit through all the coming
years. It seems to be forgotten by many persons
that this is not the first time our party has
deemed it best to support an outsider, as it were,
for Governor, and this too when the dark clouds
of business depression were not lowering over
our State.

"The Republican party is not a cast iron institution, it is reasonable, flexible, liberal and
patriotic, and has given an example of wisdom
and devotion to Texas in this matter of which
every Republican has cause to feel proud.

"In conclusion let me say: The Republican party
has clothed itself with a new dignity which should
be worn by every member of it with pride and
pleasure. At a single stride you have gone to the

very front of the procession with a compact
organization of one hundred thousands votes;
you have subordinated all personal ambition
and, prompted by patriotism alone, have laid
your offering at the feet of Texas, that she might
live. Your action challenges the admiration of
the world and the applause of your countrymen;
you have served notice on ignorance, stupidity
and prejudice that you are not to be cajoled
nor caught with any by-play of affectionate
solicitude for your welfare, when the very mischief which the administration declares its intention to subdue, has been raised and cruelly
enacted in many parts of our State, because the
powers now at Austin are wanting in ability, or
disposition, or both so to rule Texas that such
disorder would be impossible. We want a Governor whose administration will prevent wrong,
not one whose friends incite it and then declare
he will hunt down the evil doers and repair the
wrong. What reparation can be made to the
orphan and the widow? They fool us sometimes,
but cannot do so all the time.

"And let me say here that under our system
of government there is no power lodged in the
Governor to stop lynching. He can call out the
militia, and shoot down the mob if they refuse
to disperse, but the lynchers do their work
quietly and retire to their homes and if the community is in sympathy with them THAT IS THE

LAW. The only way to stop lynching is to build up a healthy public sentiment all over the State, which will condemn it as a crime against the law, humanity and God.

"What I have been to you and the party in the past twenty-two years of my public life I shall be to you in the future. Every hope we have is interwoven with the life of Texas. 'Let us have peace,' and through industry and education and loyalty to our home make it what God and nature designed it—the grandest common-wealth of them."

Discussing a brief which Gov. Hogg submitted to the people, the Galveston *News,* in an editorial of Oct. 2d, said: "Whatever may be said of Mr. Cuney, his language in public discussion is notably that of a gentleman. Admitting that Cuney, Clark and their respective adherents were willing, in a mortally dangerous emergency, to meet each other half way as patriotic citizens to rescue and redeem Texas, if need be at the sacrifice of their respective parties, where is the reproach of such subordination of love of party to love of country in such an emergency? Is it opprobrious for Texans to be first of all for the salvation of Texas?"

The Colorado (Texas) *Times* said: "Of late the Galveston *News* seems to have a mighty fine opinion of the Republicans—it depends upon them to save the State! And with the Negro at the head of that party too? Lord, upon what evil times have we fallen!"

The *News* immediately replied: "You have survived them a good while. The Negro vote has controlled Colorado County ever since the war."

This contest for Governor was one of the most exciting ever held in the State. Senator Coke started the battle cry for Hogg, with the slogan of the three C's—"Clark, Cuney, and the Coons." There were no dull moments in the campaign. Father constantly traveled, making many political speeches. Souvenirs of the campaign found their way to our home; one the tall gray hat, insignia of the Clark followers.

It was rightfully charged that the Negroes were supporting Gov. Hogg. A number of the colored Republican voters could not be persuaded to vote for a Democrat, though the candidate be a Progressive, while in a few cases, the motive, unfortunately, was not that of party loyalty. The Populist party, in the State as in the country at large, made further division of the vote of the two old parties, and thus the State was carried for the regular Democrats by Governor Hogg.

In 1893, when Grover Cleveland had been inaugurated President of the United States, and the appointment of father's successor for Collector of Customs was expected, the representative men of the city, Democrats and Republicans, sent a petition to the Secretary of the Treasury at Washington, asking for his retention as long as a Democratic administration could consistently maintain him there, and added, "We owe it to fairness and candor, to say that the office has been managed admirably; in every department the utmost courtesy has always been shown, and where needed, willing aid to facilitate our business with promptness, intelligence and care. Some of us endorsed Mr. Cuney at the time of his appointment; all of us endorse him as an able and faithful servant at the approach of his probable retirement."

The signatures appended were those of men who represented the wealth and business interests of the District, and their friendly act of endorsement, under the circumstances, was greatly commented on.

At the appointment of his Democratic successor, father retired from office with the good will and best wishes of all the patrons of the Custom House. After leaving official life, father continued the business of stevedoring. Later, entering the business of building contracting, he became one of the firm of Clark and Company. Among the buildings contracted for and erected were the Waller County Court House and the M. E. (White) Church of Houston, regarded as one of the finest structures in the State..

On the first of January, 1893, I wrote father

of a visit I had made to the night schools of Cambridge, Mass., with a friend who taught there in the schools. I was impressed with the helpfulness of the work and asked if something could not be done toward the establishment of night schools in Galveston.

The last Census enumeration had brought out the fact that one-third of the children of Galveston within scholastic age, could not attend the day schools. Many worked at home or were employed in the Santa Fe shops and the cotton mill. There were older people too—men and women of color who had lacked opportunity in youth, to whom the schools would prove beneficial.

On January 8th father wrote me, "I sent you the *News* to-day which will show you that your papa has acted on the suggestion of his dear little girl about the Public Night School. Think of what a loyal little Galvestonian you are—to you and you alone will be due this great service to humanity and the place that gave you birth. How proud I am of you, my dear one. The whole city is alive with the idea. I shall push it for all there is in it for you, dear."

And again January 9th: "I wrote you yesterday but failed to send the clipping from the *News* of that date. I shall send you everything of importance that takes place relating to the night school. I am very hopeful of having your suggestion put into effect by the first of next month."

A clipping from the Galveston *News* of Feb. 2d read: "February first 1893, three free night schools were established in Galveston by the Board of School Trustees. The attendance, double what had been expected, demonstrated the need of these institutions." There were two schools for white and one for colored pupils. Much praise is due Pres. R. B. Hawley of the school board and Supt. Cooper, who made the result possible.

CHAPTER XVII.

LINING UP FOR BATTLE.

DURING the following year, there were suspicious actions on the part of those who were supposed to wield powerful influence within the Republican party, that led to the belief that there were plans on foot to make another strong effort to turn the party organization over to the alien body—the "Lily White" Republicans.

In an interview on April 16, 1894, Hon. N. B. Moore, Chairman of the State Republican Executive Committee, asserted of the "Lily Whites" that "there were no better or more patriotic Republicans in the State than the men who differed with us in 1892. These men will re-unite with us. It is going to be but little trouble for us to harmonize. Representatives of the opposing factions have conferred with me and in every instance, I have found them, like us, anxious for a settlement of the differences upon some basis honorable alike to all, and humiliating to none. Of the result, I feel assured."

The "Lily White" Republicans, with the prospects of re-union, perfected their plans for party

167

control in the State. In May, Chairman Goodell of the State "Lily White" Republican Executive Committee, issued a call indorsing the "census plan" of organization, frankly proclaiming "the idea is to separate the races in primaries as they are in schools, churches and railroads, and to give them a fixed and certain representation."

Father was asked by a *News* reporter, what he inferred from the condition of affairs. He replied: "In the Republican party there are no factions. There may be differences of opinion upon questions of party policy, but we have but one organization. All our differences will be adjusted in the convention hall.

"There is no common ground upon which the Republicans can stand with the 'Lily Whites.' That party has but one element of faith, namely: 'That the Negro shall always remain in a state of tutelage, immature and unfit to exercise any political privilege but that of blindly voting the party ticket, or furnishing the victims at election riots and supplying the article for sectional hatred. Any assumption of independent political thought is offensive to the 'Lily White' and any Negro pretending to distinction in the party is met with furious denunciation.' who can say the Negro is Republican for the office? He evidently does not get them.

"The basis of representation has always been

the vote for president at the preceding election. I do not believe there will be any departure from that rule this year.

"But I may say to you that I have letters from many friends which they have received from 'Lily Whites' and their co-adjutors in the party, urging what they term the 'census plan' of representation. According to this scheme, representation in our State shall be divided between the whites and the Negroes in a ratio shown by the census of 1890, to exist between the races in the State, irrespective of party affiliation. The proposition, in my mind, is an unqualified absurdity. It is unnecessary and unjust; unjust because it gives unmerited and paramount influence to the minority of the party, not achieved by intellectual and moral superiority. Unnecessary, because the whites have always out-numbered the Negroes in our State Conventions."

A week later, Goodell said: "I have read the recent interview of N. W. Cuney, the late colored leader, and note his usual appeal to the prejudice of his race, but it is also evident that he has directed his attention to the handwriting on the wall and realizes that, like Othello, his occupation will soon be gone.

"There seems to be a general desire for harmony in the Republican party, but just what steps will be taken, if any, during the convention of the State League of Republican Clubs

on June 12th, I am unable to state. It is belived
that the occasion will witness a gathering of
the wisdom and brains and energy of the party
such as has not been seen for years, and it is
possible that from the wisdom and lofty patriotism assembled there may emanate some plan
by which a reconciliation may be effected and
the party strengthened for the battles of the
future.   Cuney's presence will undoubtedly
have a large influence upon some members of
Judge Moore's committee, who have hitherto
been accustomed to his manipulation, but I
believe the majority of the white leaders and
the better element of the colored people have,
for some time past, been quietly undergoing a
change of sentiment in regard to the effect of
Cuney's control upon the future prospects of
the Republican party of Texas."

Father was not a member of the Republican
State Committee, but he had been named in the
Galveston County convention held Aug. 21, as
a delegate to the State convention which was to
meet at Dallas.

Differences had risen between the colored Republicans of the county over the representation
in the State convention, but with the exception
of a few disgruntled members who attempted
an ineffective split, the trouble was amicably
adjusted. This was not difficult since the two
wings were attached to the same principles.   The

final compromise was the one originally proposed by the Cuneyites; the anti-Cuney faction accepted the chairmanship and two-thirds of the Executive Committee, while they conceded two-thirds of the Dallas delegation to the Cuney wing.

The State convention met at Dallas on Aug. 28th, with about 800 delegates in attendance. In the opening address made by chairman N. B. Moore, he asked that the "Lily Whites" return to the fold and extended them a welcome. The first cry of fusion, strange to say, came from a Negro delegate, L. M. Sublett, the colored Hogg leader of McLennan County. He was answered by a spontaneous cry of "No fusion! No fusion! Put him out!"

In the session held by the Executive Committee to perfect temporary organization, Webster Flanagan, candidate of the Cuney wing, was defeated by the anti-Cuneyite, Wilbur F. Crawford, who was named as temporary chairman.

This first defeat for the Cuneyites was followed by one which was considered more disastrous. During the afternoon session, the appointment of Committees on Permanent Organization, Credentials, and Platforms and Resolutions were announced by Mr. Crawford. In reply to protests, he stated that he had appointed those he deemed the wisest. But one member of the Committee on Credentials was said to be known as friendly to father. Prospects looked bright for the friends of "harmonious re-union."

At the close of the day's proceedings, the press with flaring head-lines of "Black eye for Cuney," reported that "Cuney was routed, foot, horse and dragon!"

On the following day, when the convention assembled, the Committee on Permanent Organization reported the appointment of Webster Flanagan as permanent chairman. He was received with a splendid ovation. Much time was consumed by the report of the Committee on Credentials and the subsequent decision of contests. William H. McDonald, a young colored Republican of Kaufman County, who was now rising into prominence, carried his point in the Navarre case. The fight between the Rentfro and Maris factions was decided favorably for Rentfro and, after a sharp fight, the Galveston County (Cuney) delegation was seated.

A motion was made to nominate a State ticket. Judge Wm. K. Makemson of Williamson received the nomination for Governor by acclamation. R. B. Rentfro was nominated for Lieutenant-Governor, while A. H. Colwell, a colored delegate of Brazos, was nominated for Supt. of Public Instruction.

In a letter written by Hon. Charles W. Ogden of San Antonio in which he declined the use of his name as nominee for Goverment, he stated that he "did not agree with the ideas upon party organization entertained by the 'Lily Whites,' yet it seemed that every true Republican ought to co-operate to bring about a perfect and harmonious re-union of all Republicans in the State."

It was now seen, however, that the complexion of the convention was changing and the "census plan," which had created so much discussion, was discarded as impracticable.

The big fight of the convention came during the night session, over the Chairmanship of the Executive Committee. Father, who felt that it was dangerous longer to retain Judge Moore in the important position of State Chairman, was represented in the fight by the candidacy of Dr. John Grant of Sherman—the Republican candidate for Congress from his district in 1892. Father's enemies, together with Charles Ferguson and his brother Henry, fought for the re-election of Judge Moore.

The press reported the closing scene of the Convention as follows: "R. B. Hawley of Galveston proceeded formally to put Grant's name before the Convention. A. H. Colwell seconded the nomination and said that to defeat him would be to put the seal of condemnation upon the greatest Negro in Texas or any other State. The calls for Cuney became uproarious, and he

finally appeared upon the platform to the delight
of his friends who gave him a rousing reception.
Cuney proceeded to second the nomination of Dr.
Grant and incidentally branched off in a scathing arraignment of the present machine."

Other speeches followed, in which the convention was urged "not to be carried away by the
siren's voice nor driven by the whip." When the
roll was called it was found that Dr. Grant
was elected Chairman of the State Executive
Committee by a vote of 368 to 247. Wm. Edgar
Easton, a colored Republican and friend of
father, was named Secretary of the State Committee.

The press head-lines were changed to read:
"The Black and Tans, led by Wright Cuney,
won everything they fought for in the Convention. The permanent organization of the convention, the State ticket personnel, the Executive
Committee management for the next two years
were all shaped to Cuney's liking. His opponents discovered that Cuney could not be downed
and the fight against him for the time being
was abandoned."

It was known that father was not without
enemies within his own race, and this fact
caused the *Echo,* of Jan. 2, 1895, to say: "The
man who attempts to belittle Cuney to reach the
climax of his own ambition as Republican leader
of this State, injures his cause, destroys sym-

pathy and becomes a wreck as soon as his selfish purposes are made known, for Cuney is woven and interwoven into the very hearts of the people of Texas. His name is a by-word in the home of every Negro in the State. What Mr. Cuney is to-day, it will take the life time of more than one man, for any other Negro in the State to reach."

In February of this year occurred the death of the statesman and noted man of color, Frederick Douglass. Father delivered the oration at the memorial services held in Galveston. He had an unbounded admiration for Mr. Douglass, whom he considered not only a great moral and social reformer, but one of the greatest men of his time.

On March 26th father was nominated for Senator from the Seventeenth Senatorial District, an honor which he declined. His business now demanded considerable travel in the State and political matters required thought and attention, yet he found time for active interest in the founding of an Orphan's Home for colored children at Mexia, and to consider the needs and progress of the colored educational institutes in the State.

In June, when I returned home for my vacation from the Conservatory in Boston, via the Mallory Line from New York, I was disappointed to see father alone on the wharf to meet me. While impatiently awaiting the docking of the steamer, I called out greetings to father and asked; "Where is Mother—how is she?"

I could not catch his reply, but noticed that he turned his head away. I was afraid—and my heart ached. Mother had suffered for years from tuberculosis, but enjoying yearly travel and tenderest care, she was always cheerful and active, and was always first to welcome me after a long absence.

Mother greeted me at the door of our home— she was making a brave effort, for my sake, to be herself, but I immediately saw that her health was now in a condition to cause anxiety.

The atmosphere of Galveston is heavy and damp, so we did not remain long at home. A visit to San Antonio, in the western part of the State, had proven beneficial before, and here, to our great joy, mother rapidly improved.

Life was very happy there. San Antonio, a piece bitten out of Old Mexico, is full of an old, quaint charm. The people are lovable and my mother who was still a young woman, was the dearest of companions.

When we had been there a number of weeks, a friend persuaded us to take a little journey to Mexico. We were not very far from that country—a night's journey brought us to the Mexican border. We visited Monterey, Topo Chico Springs and Saltillo. Mother enjoyed the wonderful gardens in the midst of the foot-hills of the Sierra Madre mountains, but she grew no stronger. We returned shortly to San Antonio, where father came often to see us. The San Antonio *Express,* with other local papers, lost sight of his private life, and discussing his purpose in coming to the city, declared it was to bolster up his political power.

Leaving San Antonio for Austin, a city almost as well known as a health resort, mother and I attended the Teacher's State Convention. We lingered in Austin, for mother grew weaker, and knowing it to be impossible for her to return to Galveston, father took a cottage that she might have home comfort during her illness.

She steadily grew worse, and on October first, at the age of 39 years, she died. Father was crushed and so utterly heart-broken that the final arrangements for our sad return to Galveston were necessarily completed by me.

I have no fitting words with which to pay tribute to my mother. It was written of her, "She was charitable, sincere, strongly cognizant of duties assigned her in the proper training and education of her children. Matched with a master man, she was no less than a promoter of his welfare and a counselor in his endeavors. She possessed a deep, abiding interest in his success and shared it to the end."

CHAPTER XVIII.

The First Defeat.

Before many months had passed father was hurled into one of the most bitter contests of his life. Anticipating the campaign of 1896, he supported Wm. B. Allison of Iowa, against Wm. McKinley of Ohio for the nomination.

James S. Clarkson of Iowa, loyal and of abiding friendship, was working for Mr. Allison's interests in the East. The McKinley forces were under the leadershinp of Marcus A. Hanna. Mr. Croley in his recent biography of Mr. Hanna states that in 1895, "Mr. Hanna rented a house in Thomasville, Georgia, where he and Mr. McKinley met all comers, regardless of color, and collared the Southern delegates on the quiet." But Mr. Hanna found it impossible to swerve Wright Cuney of Texas; a fact that Mr. Hanna did not forget when he acted as Chairman of the National Committee during the McKinley campaign.

It was Mr. Hanna's desire that the management, in Texas, of the McKinley candidacy for the presidential nomination, should be in the hands of father. In March, 1895, Joseph P. Smith wrote father from Newport:

"Am here with Governor McKinley as guest of Hon. M. A. Hanna, of Cleveland, who asks me to write and extend you a most cordial invitation to visit him here prior to Wednesday, March 20th. He desires to confer with you regarding matters of mutual interest and will be much pleased to renew the acquaintance he formed with you at the National Conventions of 1888 and 1895. Please write or wire me on receipt of this note whether you can come or not and when."

On March 16, 1895, Mr. Hanna sent father the following telegram from Thomasville, Ga.

"Can you meet General William Osborne for important political conference Pickwick Club Hotel, New Orleans, next Tuesday, March Nineteenth. Please wire answer to-day."

Father's answer was,

"My family ill in San Antonio and much as I would like to meet Gen. Osborne I dare not leave home. Would greatly like to see you here."

Thereupon Hanna wrote this letter,

"Remembering you in '84 and '88, I have felt anxious to have a talk with you about '96 and hope I may find that you are favorable to our Governor (McKinley). Jim Hill of Mississippi has been here and was going to New Orleans soon. I told him I wished he would run over

to Galveston and see you, that he might give you
my ideas as to the situation.   Jos. P. Smith,
our Ohio State Librarian, is with the Gov.
acting as his sec.   He tells me that his
wife is in Galveston on a visit to his parents
and that he is going after her some time next
month.   So you will probably see him and anything he may say to you will be 'from the book'
—I have done no missionary work in Texas as
I have had the feeling that you would be for
McKinley and I fully appreciate the value of
your leadership."

Upon his arrival in Galveston, Mr. Hill
breakfasted with father and an intimate group
of friends.   As mother was out of the city, I
acted as hostess.   I well remember Mr. Hill's
disappointment at being unable to persuade
father to join the McKinley forces.

On being informed of his attitude, Mr. Hanna
again wrote to father in the following terms:
"I will say to you frankly that I am very
anxious to have you take charge of Gov. Mc-
Kinley's interests in Texas, which I feel should
soon receive some attention.   I appreciate that
it is something of a task to fully perfect an
organization and that there would be expenses,
etc., which no one should be asked to bear alone.
Then as to the proper men from whom to ask
assistance in the several Dist's—I will gladly
co-operate in all this and write personal letters

to those whom you may suggest—where you think it would have influence. And in any other way do all I can to assist you, all contingent of course upon your willingness in the matter. I write you this in confidence because I have understood that you were friendly to Gov. McKinley. If you have seen Joe Smith he will have told you how favorable everything is for the Gov. and I assure you I can see no reason why all our hopes should not materialize. I am going home to Cleveland on Wednesday and will hope to hear from you soon."

Eventually Mr. Hanna found it necessary to place the formation of the McKinley organization in Texas in other hands, as father's alliance with the Allison supporters was firm.

For some months prior to the date of the assembling of the State Convention there were fierce struggles between the opposing elements of the party in almost every county of the State, over the election of delegates to the State Convention, as well as dissensions in the Congressional districts over the election of delegates to the National Convention.

There were rumors of combinations being made between the Allison and McKinley forces, the McKinley and Reed forces, and the Allison and Reed forces, it being recognized that no one element had sufficient strength to control the convention. Before the convention as-

sembled, the press reported: "Mr. Cuney appears
to be the central figure and no man is more
eagerly sought than he. There seems to be a
sort of concentrated fight against the noted Galvestonian, but so far he is holding his own, and
says he will stand pat, come what may."

It had been further rumored that there was
a well matured plan of the McKinley followers
to capture the convention by physical force, if
need be, and thus compel the Cuney followers
to take the attitude of bolters. The concentrated
manner in which the attack in the convention
was finally made, seemed to confirm this.

On March 24, the State Convention met at
Austin. The attendance was the largest in the
history of the party in the State. It was notice-
able for the number of intelligent young col-
ored politicians: Wm. H. McDonald, W. E.
King, S. C. McCoy, Webster Wilson, L. B.
Kinchion, M. M. Rodgers, W. H. Ellis, Emmett
J. Scott, and others, as well as the largest white
contingent ever seen at a Texas Republican
State Convention.

Among men of prominence were R. B. Rentfro, R. B. Hawley, Eugene Marshall, Wm.
K. Makemson, A. J. Rosenthal, Thad Bell, E.
H. Terrell, Webster Flanagan, C. G. Clifford
and W. B. Brush. There were McKinley emissaries too, on hand, Col. Herrick and Col. Pol-
lard, ostensibly passing through the State.

Many distinguished Democrats appeared as visitors: Ex-Gov. Hogg, Gov. Culberson, Treasurer Wortham and Adjutant General Mabry.

Prior to the calling to order of the convention, the Reed and Allison forces effected a combination. Of the ante-convention proceedings the San Antonio Express said: "Interest has been intense all day, but in the midst of it all, Cuney appears smiling and serene, and is watching every movement with an eagle eye. Presidential candidates seem to be a secondary consideration and it has narrowed down to a fight of the combined leaders against Mr. Cuney. Late last evening Cuney discovered that some of the leaders had combined against him, so after a conference between him and Chairman Grant, he threw down the gauntlet by declaring himself a candidate for Temporary Chairman."

Father's position was comprehended by his declaration: "The way to have peace, by the eternal gods, is to fight for it." Dr. Grant's attitude caused surprise, for father had made one of the hardest political fights of his life at Dallas in 1894, to give Grant the chairmanship. It was known, therefore, that Grant was under obligation to him.

"Tell Mr. Cuney I will give him one hour to withdraw as a candidate for Temporary Chairman," was Dr. Grant's reply to father's announcement of his candidacy. "This doubtless sounded grandiloquent to Grant," said the Express, "and it was proud incense to his soul, but he paid dearly for the pleasure he got from it."

Preceding the opening of the convention the Executive Committee convened. From one of the windows of father's headquarters, just opposite the building in which the State Executive Committee held their meeting, I witnessed the excited eagerness with which the vast crowds about the place awaited the reports of the deliberations of the Committee.

At the close, when it became known that the Committee had voted to recommend father as Temporary Chairman, friends surrounded him, as he appeared on the street, to convey to him the news of his victory. There were cries of "Cuney has won!" and such wild enthusiasm that he was caught up in the arms of friends and carried away amid deafening yells.

When the convention assembled, the report of the executive committee recommending father for Temporary Chairman was read. The vote in the Committee was 17 to 11. The McKinley delegates, bitter over the action of the Executive Committee and, at the same time, desiring to make a test of their strength as against the Reed-Allison combination, proposed J u d g e Rosenthal as a substitute for temporary chairman, in father's stead. A vote was at once taken by a roll call with the result that father received 574 votes to 227 for Judge Rosenthal.

The press commented: "It was a great victory, and Cuney can, with pardonable pride, congratulate himself and the men who stood so faithfully by him. It was a fight to the finish, a contest in which the very existence of the Galveston man was involved.

"Notwithstanding he had arrayed against him the combined opposition of the Republican leaders, with the exception of R. B. Hawley and one or two others, he did not shirk the gage of battle thrust upon him, but gamely picked up the gauntlet and stood to his guns.

"He was the victor in spite of the odds which he had to overcome. There is probably not another man who participated in the convention, who could have won the spurs, now worn by Cuney, in such a contest."

Ex-Gov. Hogg, who had been watchful of the proceedings, had predicted father's victory, while Treasurer Wortham laughingly remarked: "They just can't down Galveston on anything."

Prior to the re-assembling of the convention, father, proposing to treat the McKinley delegates fairly in the preparation of the lists of committees which the convention had ordered him to appoint, sent to Dr. Grant, as leader of the McKinley forces, and to Mr. Hawley, leader

of the Reed followers, requesting each of them
to make suggestions to him of names of members
for the various committees.

Owing to the great many contests, the Credentials Committee had a most laborious task. Out
of a total membership of thirteen there were
three or four McKinley men on the Committee.
In nearly every case passed on, however, the
cases were settled by a practically unanimous
vote. Up to the time of the final adjournment of
the committee, there had been no mention of
a minority report.

On the re-assembling of the convention, it
was found that the McKinley delegates had, as
was rumored, entered the hall and taken possession of the prominent seats immediately in front
of the platform, enabling them seriously to obstruct the proceedings. The report of the Committee on Credentials was presented and a motion for its adoption was made by Eugene Marshall of Dallas, and promptly seconded.

Some one then offered to present a minority
report; as no minority report had been made
when the committee adjourned, and as it was
learned that the so-called minority report had
been prepared subsequently to the final adjournment of the Credentials Committee, by
delegates who were not members of the committee, the temporary chairman declared it out
of order, stating that the only question before

the house was the adoption or rejection of the unanimous report of the committee.

He further suggested that if it was desired to discuss the report of the committee, half an hour should be given to each side, and that then a vote should be taken on the adoption of the report.

The McKinley delegates, noisy and boisterous, repeatedly demanded the so-called minority report. The delegates of the Reed and Allison combination constantly clamored for a roll call on the previous question, but the McKinley men defiantly shouted that a roll call should not be had, and then with noisy demonstrations, attempted to block the proceedings of the convention.

The chairman put the motion for a viva voce vote on the previous question. The motion was at last adopted. The McKinley delegates laid much stress on this question of a so-called minority report of the Committee on Credentials, and the refusal of the chairman to receive it, and charged that father was arbitrary and unfair in his ruling.

While these preceedings were going on in the convention there was much confusion and, on the part of the McKinley delegates, yells and interruptions. It was now plainly seen that the opposition to the combination, bitter over their defeat, was determined to obstruct the work

of the convention and by violent methods prevent any action.

E. H. Terrell, W. K. Makemson, Henry C.
Ferguson and father were elected delegates-at-
large to the National Convention, and C. D.
Keyes, F. W. Gross, J. C. Cain and R. B. Smith
were elected alternates-at-large.

The Committee on Permanent Organization
made a unanimous report by which father
was made permanent chairman of the convention, in spite of the fact that there were
a number of McKinley delegates on the committee. A motion to endorse the candidacy of
Gov. McKinley for the presidential nomination
was defeated.

The McKinley delegates now attempted to
take violent posssession of the stage, seize the
chairman's table and forcibly take possession
of the convention. It was actually necessary
for the police of the city to interfere and compel
the delegates to return to their seats.

On the adjournment of the convention, the
McKinley followers, a group of 250 or 300 men,
without credentials of any kind, immediately
held a convention. Richard Allen, colored, of
Harris county, was made temporary chairman.
John Grant, Frank Hamilton, R. L. Smith, and
Dr. W. E. Davis were elected delegates to the
National Convention at St. Louis. The delegates
were instructed to vote for Gov. McKinley and

were determined to claim seats in the National Convention, as the regular elected delegates-at-large. When the convention was over, father, who never once during the hard ordeal lost his composure, showed signs of intense physical and mental strain. For three days he had worked almost incessantly and, having very little time for sleep, he now plainly showed that he was suffering from want of rest. I awaited him at his headquarters, and insisted upon his resting. Yielding to my wishes, he received the many delegations that came to congratulate him, in the room to which we had retired for quiet.

A handsome gavel was presented to father, when he was elected chairman of the convention, by James B. Sargent of Orange County. The gavel is a remembrance of that sensational struggle which I have treasured. It is emblematic—made of gum-camphor wood, grown in Orange County, the handle of Texas bamboo, and the gavel itself encased in white and black bands, one on either side, indicative of the white and black races. It has also gold and silver rims, representing bimetalism.

While admiring the gavel, father called to introduce me to the delegations as they were about to bid him good-bye. At this time an amusing and, to me, embarrassing incident occurred. Among the Delegates was Mr. B.,

lately of Chicago, with whom father had had an
altercation at the Chicago convention in 1884,
but who was now friendly toward him.   As a
reminder of his identity, father, turning to me
said in an undertone "formerly of the Gazette,
you know."   It then dawned upon me just who
the gentleman was, and I exclaimed with the
thoughtlessness of youthful pride: "Oh, and I
have the cane yet"—the weapon with which
father had worsted him in the fight.   I had no
sooner spoken than I realized the unkindness of
such a reminder.   The delegates, amused at my
discomfiture, saved the situation by bursting into
roars of laughter, in which they were joined
by father and even Mr. B. himself.

The contest resulting from the two State conventions was carried to the St. Louis Convention.   There were many conjectures as to the
outcome.   The majority felt that the regular
delegates-at-large would be sustained.

Mr. George M. Pridgen, a prominent Republican of Cuero, said: "I am unable to compre-
hend how any men pretending to be intelligent
and honorable, could go into a convention in
good faith and lend their assistance in electing
a temporary chairman to preside over them,
thereby expressing their confidence in his honesty and integrity, and raise a howl after they
fail to gain their point.

"Cuney's victory was simply the result of

brain versus boodle, and Cuney will be sustained by the St. Louis Convention. The best lawyers in Austin say Cuney's rulings as temporary chairman were in accord with strict rudiments of parliamentary tactics."

Mr. McDonald, a colored delegate of prominence, said: "They may talk about Cuney all they want to, but Cuney did not buy votes as the McKinley men did. They are busy now paying off the delegates they bought last night. They were shrewd enough, however, not to pay the money until they had secured the goods, and for this I give them credit. I never in all my life saw anything more bold and yet they are the cattle that are abusing Mr. Cuney."

Previous to the convention, father had said to a reporter of the San Antonio Express: "They have not enough money to buy the convention against me. I am going before the next legislature to ask for the enactment of a law which will put in the penitentiary every man who tries to bribe a delegate."

Before going to St. Louis, father visited Washington, D. C. He had long been interested and hopeful for the success of Howard University, the institution for colored youth founded by Gen. O. O. Howard which is situated in that city.

It was due to his efforts, through friends in Congress, that the University was given necessary appropriation, and continued to be a Government school.

In appreciation of his "mastery of the arts of high living and noble thinking" he was given by Howard University, at the commencement in 1896, the honorary degree of Master of Arts.

CHAPTER XIX.

The National Convention of 1896.

On June 16th, the Republican National Convention met at St. Louis, Missouri. Among the visitors of national reputation were the following colored Americans: Ex-Senator B. K. Bruce, Ex-Congressman John R. Lynch, Ex-Governor P. B. S. Pinchback, Gen. Robert Smalls, Congressman George W. Murray, Col. Perry Carson and Prof. R. R. Wright. It was noted, however, that they were taking little or no part in the proceedings of the convention. At no former convention had the colored man been so inconspicuous.

Prominent among the party leaders were Gen. Foraker, Gen. Lew Wallace, Matthew Quay, Thomas Platt, Senator Lodge, Garrett Hobart, Gen. Alger, R. L. Kerens and Mark Hanna. Gen. James S. Clarkson, who was very ill in Philadelphia, was sadly missed.

Father, who had arrived early, was very bitter against the St. Louis hotel proprietors who discriminated against the delegates of color. "When the question of choosing a convention city came up before the National Committee at Washington last December," he said to a representative of the press, "I opposed St. Louis because of the prejudice here against the colored man. I had had some experience at the Planters' once myself, and felt certain that every Negro who applied for admission at a St. Louis hotel at this time would receive similar treatment.

"I told friends of St. Louis there, that I had no objection to their city, and that I preferred it as a convention city to Chicago, Washington, Pittsburgh or San Francisco, in all respects. Three St. Louis hotel men, the proprietors of three of your largest hotels, including the Planters' and Southern, came to me and pledged me that if St. Louis got the convention they would see that the doors of the best hotels of the city were opened to black as well as white delegates.

"One of the three deciding votes on the fourth ballot was cast by myself. I changed from San Francisco to St. Louis, with two others, and the convention is to be held here in consequence.

"I believe the gentlemen of your local committee, as a whole, acted in good faith in making those promises, but you see the result. St. Louis will be injured more than you would suppose by this failure to keep its promises."

At the meeting of the National Committee during convention week, this matter was brought up with the result that the Southern, Laclede, St. Nicholas and Lindell hotels agreed to accommodate the colored delegates.

On June 15th, before the opening of the convention, the Grant delegates held a meeting which was composed entirely of McKinley men. Being anti-Cuney in sentiment, Dr. Grant was elected for the position of National Committeeman for the State of Texas.

On June 17th, the Texas contest came before the National Committee, which was controlled by McKinley men. The decision was against the delegates elected in the regular State convention. The McKinley men had captured the Credentials Committee, and their control was confirmed when a resolution offered by Hepburn of Iowa, one of the Allison supporters, that the committee send for the papers in all contests, was lost.

Among the 58 contests brought before the Credentials Committee, was that of Texas. The action of the National Committee was, of course, confirmed. The Allison-Reed delegates-at-large were unseated by a vote of 31 to 20 and the McKinley delegates recognized. Father's disappointment was keen and was aggravated by the fact that he was treated unfairly.

In the National Committee, Gen. Grosvenor

of Ohio, the "official calculator of the McKinley campaign," at a moment of father's absence when he knew father would have no opportunity to reply to his cowardly assault, made in his speech of opposition to the Allison-Reed delegates, a personal attack accusing father of political dishonesty.

Mr. Thomas Fortune of New York, who saw father just after the happening, said: "Grosvenor's attack was for twelve hours the talk of St. Louis among the assembled Republican hosts, for it was known that Cuney was always the soul of political honor.

"Congressman Grosvenor is an old man, with long gray hair, and flowing beard. He may not know it, but he owes it to me, that he was not publicly whipped in the streets of St. Louis. Soon after he had made his terrific arraignment of Cuney, I met the latter at Planters' hotel. The Black Flagger was trembling with suppressed rage and indignation, and his brown eyes fairly blazed in his head. Cuney's eyes were most expressive. In repose they were insistently nervous and restless; under any sort of excitement they fairly danced. The African, Indian and Anglo-Saxon blood in him formed a combination which made him almost invincible in a fair fight of whatever sort. Indeed, he was a man of fierce courage.

"Cuney declared in his cool, deliberate way

that Gen. Grosvenor had attacked him and had
done him a mortal injustice and that he proposed to whip him. We reasoned the matter out
and Cuney finally accepted my view, although
with very great reluctance as the injustice rankled in his soul."

Father's indignation was emphasized by his
speech before the Committee on Credentials;
"Turn me out, and you not only place the brand
of dishonor upon the Republican party of the
nation, you not only do the act of petty revenge-
ful tyrants, but you put upon ingratitude, that
lowest vice of inhuman hearts, a premium.

"You make the deed of Judas Iscariot a grand
and noble performance.

"That ex-inmate of a lunatic asylum," he continued, pointing to Grant, "is my creature. I
warmed him into life. He betrayed and stung
me. Look at him as he sits there with a face
as white as the linen you cannot see and
a heart as black as the coat that conceals it.
He is my creature. I made him. I stood by
him when he had not a friend. I gave him a
chance to come to the front and held him up
against the protests of my friends. And all the
time he has been plotting to undermine me.

"With a backing of the subsidizing wing of
the Republican party, he has come here with
lies upon his lips, and you, gentlemen, are in-
clined to take his words against the testimony

of men who have taken the wounds and fought
the battles of the Republican party when he was
voting the Democratic ticket.

"For twenty years I have stood in the van
and taken all the blows of the enemy in a State
where it costs men a great deal more to stand
up for their political convictions than it does
in Gen. Grosvenor's State.

"For ten years I have served as National
Committeeman from Texas in the councils of
the Republican party. My word has been taken
as lightly by this body as if I were a raw re-
cruit, a discredited stranger, a man of no standing.

"Let me tell you, gentlemen, you may go to
my political enemies in the city where I have
spent all my years since I became a man, and
they will tell you that Wright Cuney's name
stands as a synonym for commercial integrity
and for personal honor; that he has never broken
a law against good citizenship, good fellowship
and humanity since he has lived among them,
and that any and every Democrat of property
in the community in which he lives, is willing
to go on his bond. Can the upstart," (pointing
to Grant), "show a like record?

"But waiving personalities, I stand on the
broad ground of right. I, and my fellow delegates, have shown a title to our seats by every
rule of right procedure. If you strike us down,

you do it because we have dared to assert our manhood by daring to support the minority candidates in the convention. You may stab me and my colleagues, but remember when you do, the knife may rebound and enter the vitals, not only of the Republican cause in Texas, but that of the nation as well."

Indicative of the sentiment in the State of Texas, regarding the unseating of the Allison-Reed delegates, was the following editorial which appeared in one of the largest Democratic dailies of Texas, The San Antonio *Express:* "N. W. Cuney, the colored Republican leader of Texas, met with an unkind fate in St. Louis. He has been downed, but not at home.

"The entire Republican party of Texas was unable to cope with his energy, influence or generalship. It was only through an accident of politics that his enemies were able to call to their assistance the national leaders and dethrone, temporarily, at least, the sable statesman. Viewed from a non-partisan standpoint, and without race prejudice, Cuney was entitled to a seat in the St. Louis convention. He had the Republican organization with him. Had there been nothing at stake for the McKinley managers in St. Louis, little reason would have been found why Cuney and his friends should not have been accorded the fruits of their labors. As it is, he is thrown out simply be-

cause of his fidelity to a minority candidate,
and to make more room for the McKinley forces.

"There was a world of truth in the few remarks addressed by Cuney to his late white
admirers, and these words will not soon be forgotten. Such things stick in the craw of a
Southern white man of any spirit, and the time
for harmony about which Mr. Grant talks so
glibly has gone by. It will be a war to the
knife and the knife to the hilt, and Cuney will
wield the machete with a skill born of the
darker half of his ancestry.

"Cuney is not dead politically. He will live
to attend the political funeral of several of the
politicians who traded him out of his rights at
the St. Louis convention.

"A man who will stick by his friends at the risk
of his own future, is made of no common clay,
be it white or black. Cuney could have been
seated as a delegate had he so willed it. The
McKinleyites would have joyfully hailed his ac-
cession to their ranks.

"Cuney had his friends to carry and his
promises to keep. He carried his friends and
went down with the ship. He kept his promises
and was derided for so doing. Many a white
politician could adopt his method with advantage to himself and the party he represents.

"It is well for the Republican party in Texas
that a move now has been made towards the rec-

lamation of the party from the hands of the
Negro leadership, but it is a strange commen-
tary upon the remarkable strength of such
leadership when the party was forced to go out
of the State and adopt such questionable methods
to accomplish it."

Further opinion of men of national repute
concerning the result of the Texas contest, can
be gleaned from a portion of a letter written
to father by a friend of Pres. McKinley: "I
find that the animosities engendered at St.
Louis during our alleged convention, are gradu-
ally wearing off. Major Dick, who is Hanna's
right hand man, has a better understanding of
Texas matters (men and issues), and there are
several very close to Gov. McKinley who do
not approve of much that was done at St. Louis."

Through correspondence from the same source
father was told in a letter of July 31: "Sinclair
(Postmaster at Galveston) gave Hanna a strong
talk in your behalf and made a decided impres-
sion on him as regards your personality and
reliability. I heard the talk, and Hanna had
been filled with so many lies, he evinced surprise to hear all that Sinclair said; he told
Hanna in the plainest of English that Gen.
Grosvenor's conduct was nothing short of an
outrage, both indecent and unjust, and he (Grosvenor) would live to regret it.

"Major Dick is your friend, and away down

in his boots. Gen. Payne of Wisconsin only
awaits an opportunity to give you some signal
recognition. I hope that you are not living in
the events that are behind. The political world
is moving fast, very fast, and it seems to me,
that a great opportunity is opening to you."

Immediately after the adjournment of the
National Convention, father went to Hot
Springs, Ark., for rest. While there, he received a letter intimating that a reconciliation
was desired on the part of his opponents. It
read, in part: "Your friends feel deeply with
you the wound which the National Committee
inflicted upon you in its session in St. Louis,
and they appreciate what a gallant and noble
fight you made before them. They also feel
that their opinions as to your future action are
worthy of consideration, and should be of material weight with you. That you should be influenced by their advice is not presuming too
much, for they have your best interests at heart
as well as the welfare of the party. We believe that the fiercest battles of the campaign
will be fought on the fields of Illinois and Indiana, and for you to enlist your services for the
fight, buckle on your armor and go forth to
battle will not be expecting too much of you, a
man accustomed to lead and to fight where the
battle wages fiercest. We believe that you can
be of inestimable value to the party by offer-

ing your services to the party at this time, when they are most needed.

"If agreeable to your views, we will set to work to bring about that which we have suggested and only await your approval and acquiescence. We believe, if you so prefer, negotiations to that end will come from your former opponents."

Father resented the injustice which had been done him, and accepted with great reluctance, the result of the contest. He refused, however, to "sulk in his tent," and entered the campaign for McKinley and Hobart.

Hon. John Grant, the newly elected National Committeeman, who was soon found in conference with the "Lily White" faction stated that he saw no necessity for two Republican parties in Texas, with the National organization on the eve of a great battle and with victory in sight.

"From now on," he added, "there will be a united party in Texas."

J. A. Baker, a prominent "Lily White" declared: "We have about decided to return to the regular camp and assist Grant in advancing the best interests of Republicanism in Texas."

CHAPTER XX.

THE LAST DAYS.

It was early known that there was to be a fight made on father at the coming State convention, and that much depended upon the outcome. In the event of father's ultimate victory, there would be no union with the Lily Whites.

On Sept. 9th, at Fort Worth, the State convention was held. It was one of importance, for the Republicans held the balance of power and could practically say who should control the State Government after the coming election. Whatever the differences between the Grant and Cuney factions, each had in mind the success of the party.

Father advocated fusion with the Populists, since the combined vote of the two parties was far greater than that of the Democrats. On Aug. 16th, he had received a communication from the National headquarters, asking information concerning his Fusion projects.

On the scene when convention day arrived, were the two Hanna emissaries, Gen. A. W. Huston, National Committeeman from In-

diana and Charles Hedges, of the Chicago branch
of the National headquarters. Their appearance at the Fort Worth headquarters was criticised by a number of the delegates, which
caused Gen. Huston to say: "Not for the world
would I interfere with your local self-government. The man who thinks I am against Cuney
is mistaken. I know he has done valuable service for the Republican party in Texas. I know
he was treated badly at St. Louis.

"I am not insisting on the man who has a
majority of votes in this convention, retiring in
favor of a man who has a minority of the votes.
I appreciate Cuney. He is unquestionably the
choice of the delegates here for Chairman, therefore I say let's elect him. Above all things, I
am not against him."

Among the arriving delegates, was Cecil Lyon,
of suspicious Lily White sympathies, who was
making a strong fight for Grant. There were
also among the Cuney enemies, a number of
men of color, including Richard Allen of Houston and Charles Ferguson. Of the latter, who
now again had changed his affiliation, the representative of the Galveston *News,* said: "I have
watched Ferguson with interest, but will have
to quit him. These frequent flops are injurious
in warm weather. They might bring on heart
failure."

This remark can be better understood when

it is explained that, in 1895, Mr. Ferguson returned from a meeting of Republican League
Clubs held in Cleveland, Ohio, committed to Mc-
Kinley's candidacy. Later, in the Fourth Congressional District Campaign, he was a Reed
contestant. In opposition to Grant, he fought
with the Allison-Reed combination; after arriving at the St. Louis convention, he became a
McKinley man. Being repulsed by some of
the leaders there, he was, for a short while, a
strong anti-Grant man. Now, after the close
of that contest, we find him supporting Mr.
Grant. From now on, he and his brother, Henry
Ferguson, favored opposite factions in the party.

The day preceding the opening of the convention, the press reported: "It is doubtful if
there ever was a party in Texas situated as is
the Republican party at this time. The rank
and file stand loyal, but await action until the
leaders arrive. The bold, defiant contingent
here, is that at the back of Cuney. As usual,
this wing is fighting on the aggressive, and as
fast as his friends arrive they are announcing
straight out for E. H. R. Green for State Chairman and Cuney for temporary chairman."

Mr. Green, President of the Texas Midland
Railroad, son of Hetty Green the famous capital-
ist of New York, had entered Texas politics a
few years before.

Mr. Green was father's choice for State Chairman of the Executive Committee. Among the Cuney-Green supporters were Dr. Wilmot, Eugene Marshall, E. H. Terrell, Wm. H. McDonald, M. M. Rodgers and many young intelligent colored voters.

In opposition to father's nomination for temporary chairman, the Executive Committee, of which Dr. Grant was chairman, recommended Charles Ferguson. A private caucus was held, when propositions were made to father to withdraw. He replied that under no circumstances would he withdraw, that he was in the fight to a finish. Again proposals for a compromise were made. He refused to listen to them. The fight was taken before the Convention, and father was defeated.

The scene was thus described by the News representative: "I have no interest in Cuney. I have no interest in Grant. Thanks to a pretty fair education and a good moral training, I have no interest in the Republican party. But when the fight came it was my duty to see it, and when it was ended 'La Paloma' with all its sadness took possession of me, and I hated to see the man die the death he did.

"It was just this way. Away back yonder—away back in the eighties, I saw this man come to the front as a leader. I saw him in many conventions, for these were battlefields where he fought, and I never saw him quail. Time and

again I saw him when I thought he must go
down. Time and again he triumphed. He received scars. He left them on those he fought.
He had a certain chivalry that commended him
to me, and at times his manner of warfare was
to a degree sublime. And thus he has gone
on, until those who had felt his blade were legion,
and the time was coming when they would pull
him down.

"He cast his fortune with Clarkson in the
last campaign for presidential nominations. Allison was the choice of Clarkson. He became
the choice of Cuney. The McKinley forces
were organizing on a strictly black flag plan.
They gave no quarter in any part of the field.
Those who desired to depose Cuney from the
head of the Republican party in this State saw
their chance. They got together in a solid
phalanx. They made the fight against him
and they had for their leaders the shrewdest
politicians in the Republican party.

"Their leaders were not Texans. Hanna and
Grosvenor and Thompson of Ohio were coun-
selors. They drew the map of the field. They
told how the moves should be made. The fight
was a hard one. For the first time in his life,
Cuney had waged a war in which there was
pure science on the other side.

"He had resorted to sentiment, of which he
had a thorough knowledge, in all fights before.

Now he ran up against the cold steel of method and business, and he went down wounded unto death at St. Louis, but game.

"And he fought with all his vigor. But the scars he had left were on the hearts of the many, and they had not forgotten them. The prize fought for was a small one. There was nothing of honor or profit in it. He went down, but he went down game—game as he had lived."

The second morning of the convention, Hon. E. H. R. Green was elected by acclamation for chairman of the State Executive Committee. Dr. Grant had hoped for re-election, but after the struggle over the temporary chairmanship, he found that the tide had set so strongly against him, that he was made to withdraw in favor of father's candidate, Mr. Green. Mr. Wm. Edgar Easton, a faithful Cuney adherent, was re-elected Secretary of the State Executive Committee and the Cuney plan of fusion with the sound money voters of the State was approved.

The platform as adopted by the convention showed that father had been successful in carrying through nearly every measure he had proposed to the convention.

Father had been defeated for the temporary chairmanship, but it was a more important victory to carry the fusion measure that he had fathered. It necessitated Dr. Grant's withdrawal from the State chairmanship contest, and forced him to acquiesce in the fusion program.

His plan was approved by the National Committee. Before the convention, father had received a letter from the National headquarters at Chicago, saying: "Texas is beginning to attract attention and Hanna and others are coming to believe that something tangible may come out of the fusion with the Populists and the sound money Democrats—you are the one man who can probably arrange this fusion."

On the last day of the Fort Worth convention, Dr. Grant sent a letter to father suggesting that they should be friends.—"I shall be glad to take your hand," he said, "and walk out on the platform and convince the convention that American manhood towers above pique. Please intimate your desires and I will meet them." There was a tentative reconciliation. With father, a public difference did not necessarily result in personal feeling.

In spite of the Lily Whites' repeatedly expressed desire for affiliation with the regular State Republican party, they were unwilling to discard "census plan," and they continued their State organization.

During the campaign, it was seen that in some unaccountable way, the control of precinct and county organization had gotten almost entirely into the hands of undesirable parties. Although without long political experience, Mr. Green was a leader of courage and under his direction, the conditions fast changed. Not long after, the press spoke of seeing the "fine Italian hand of Cuney" in the management of party affairs in the State.

After the National election, in which the Republicans were victorious, Dr. Grant insisted upon controlling the patronage in Texas. Of his demands, a correspondent wrote father from Washington: "He graciously conceded the Post Offices in my District. He is so selfish, he is so unfair, he is so unpatriotic and he is so utterly devoid of that necessary guide, common sense, that before he is through with his exactions he will be without friends in the party and without the respect of the administration, if he has not lost that already. He goes, slowly perhaps, but surely to that goal which inevitably awaits all men who forget their friends."

Before many months had passed, Dr. Grant quarrelled with Mr. Green, carrying the disagreement so far as to have himself elected in Mr. Green's stead. It was an ineffectual bolt. Dr. Grant's lengthy and erratic public letters and addresses finally gave warning of his sad misfortune—an unbalanced mind.

A gentleman who was present at a dinner

party in 1897, in Washington, given by the Vice-President to bring the Hon. Mark A. Hanna, and Gen. James S. Clarkson and the Hon. Samuel Fessenden together, has told me of an incident which illustrates quite vividly my father's high standing and proved integrity in every form and temptation of practical politics as well as in the business world.

According to this gentleman's story, just as the party was sitting down to the dinner table, Mr. Hobart, always a congenial spirit and the life of any party, had a letter handed to him by his butler. He at once handed it over to Senator Hanna, saying, "Here is a letter for you, Senator, from the South."

Mr. Hanna glanced at the letter and said: —"Oh, that's from Florida and I expect it's from so-and-so (giving the name of a leading colored politician in Florida) and he's a good fellow who helped us in the campaign for the nomination."

Mr. Hanna then turned to Mr. Hobart, and surprised all present by saying,—"Do you know, Hobart, we finally captured all the Southern Niggers, except Clarkson's, and especially that man Cuney and his followers in Texas. Nothing could touch or affect him, either in immediate performances or in future promises. Nothing could change him from Clarkson or Allison." He went on to account for these men's standing for convictions as being solely actuated by their attachment to Clarkson.

My informant said that everybody present seemed to know at once that this talk would be resented both by Clarkson and Fessenden, and Hobart immediately began to try and keep the peace, and smooth it over. But Clarkson broke out to protest against Mr. Hanna's assumption, and addressing him directly said, "Senator Hanna, when you are talking of Wright Cuney you are talking of a man of honor of life-long record, of a man who is as honorable as any man in this room, and a man whom several of us here have known intimately for many years, and prize as a personal friend. Whatever he did with you or your people in that campaign, or refused to do, was from his own high sense of honor, and he is worthy of that fact being recognized by you and every other gentleman."

My informant further said, "Mr. Fessenden fully corroborated all that Mr. Clarkson had said in his estimate of Mr. Cuney and his earnest defense of him.

"Senator Hanna soon found that there were colored men of the highest character in the Republican party, and plenty of Republican leaders to defend them; and the incident was finally closed. Yet it served to defeat the establishment of friendly relations between Hanna and Clarkson and Fessenden.

"The latter two not only resented this reflection on Mr. Cuney, but neither could forget
or fail to appreciate how often Mr. Cuney had
fairly seen to it that a clean and honorable delegation had been elected by the Texas Republican State Convention to the National Convention to support Reed, Allison and Morton.
Mr. Hanna and his following at St. Louis by
pressure on the National Committee got this
legal delegation unseated, and an illegal delegation put in its place, to vote for McKinley.
Thus Mr. McKinley's first term closed without
General Clarkson and Mr. Fessenden being
brought in to muster under Mr. Hanna, as his
allies and supporters."

A number of happy events of a social as
well as political nature had served to break the
strain of the aggressive campaign of 1896.
Large receptions were given in many of the
cities throughout the State, by colored citizens
who wished at this time to give evidence of the
esteem in which father was held.

Coming in the spring of 1897 from San
Antonio, where he had been called to deliver an
address on "The Duty of the Hour," father
stopped in Austin. My young brother Lloyd
had been placed in school at Tillotson College,
while I had charge of the Music Department of
the Deaf, Dumb and Blind Institute of the State
of Texas. Father came often to see us. His

visits were greatly enjoyed by the young blind men of the Institution, in whose progress father was deeply interested.

About this time, my pianoforte teacher, Edmund Ludwig, formerly of the Conservatory for Royal Ladies at St. Petersburg, with whom I was continuing my studies, had arranged for me a Piano Recital at the Opera House. Programs were in the hands of the printer when it dawned upon the management of the Opera House that it would not do to allow seating of white and colored patrons together. They telephoned that it would be necessary to sell tickets to colored patrons for the balconies only. Mr. Ludwig and I indignantly canceled the contract for the House. No hall being available, the recital, with the kind assistance of Mr. Ludwig, was given at the Institution.

Father enjoyed the occasion and, while I thought he was tired, he seemed less depressed. He disapproved of the custom of wearing black and, finding that my mourning garb saddened him, I discarded it whenever he came to see me.

During the Christmas holidays we were the honored guests at a reception arranged by an organization of colored citizens at Fort Worth, Texas. The Fort Worth (daily) Mail-Telegram, speaking of the enthusiastic reception accorded father, noted the influence the organization wielded politically, the progressive spirit of the membership and the significance of the occasion. "The speeches" according to this report, "were bright and well delivered. Of course Mr. Cuney was looked upon to make a happy talk and so he did. He earnestly thanked those present for the great compliment paid him and his daughter, and said at some future time he hoped to talk politics to them."

Father had been in constant demand before the election, at the many large rallies where he spoke in the interest of sound money. The Congressional campaign followed immediately.

Being desirous of sending a Republican congressman to Washington from the Tenth District, father, having refused to consider the nomination for himself, worked enthusiastically for the nominee, Hon. R. B. Hawley of Galveston. There was no white man in the State for whom he felt a deeper affection and he worked unceasingly for his success.

In the midst of his travels, he stopped for a few days in Austin. I saw that he was not well. He admitted to me that he had entered the campaign against the advice of his physician, for his health was undermined by a recent attack of grippe, of which he had kept me in ignorance. I entreated him to give up his duties and stay at Austin until his health returned. This he was reluctant to do; he was conducting the campaign, but he promised, that after fulfilling

the approaching engagements he would come
back to me and rest.

Mr. Hawley was elected to Congress. It was
noted as a significant fact that father's district,
in which he conducted the campaign, was the
only Congressional district in Texas which went
Republican.

Within a few weeks, father returned to Austin.
Here he had a relapse, which was directly caused
by speaking at outdoor meetings in his already
weakened condition. I was greatly alarmed,
and insisted upon his laying aside all political
and business cares, that he might have a long
rest in the mountains. But grief over the death
of my mother, added to the anxieties and worries
of hard campaigns, over-taxed his magnificent
vitality and only made his condition the more
serious. A troublesome cough set in. We decided to take a cottage in the mountains near
San Antonio.

In the little health resort of Boerne, in the
south-western part of the State, I fought unceasingly and desperately with death, for the
life of my idolized father.

The summer was long and intensely hot—we
drove daily in the early mornings and late in
the evenings. The papers and the magazines
were his daily companions, and under the trees
we read and talked.

He was besieged with letters from all parts

of the State and country. Many of them were good, friendly letters that I was glad to have him receive, but more of them were petitions and letters of political importance that he could not be persuaded to neglect.

I now acted as his secretary. In spite of his weakened condition, father declared that he was growing in strength and, holding his political interests, he continued through correspondence to take part in the affairs of the State.

A number of times he was called to San Antonio to attend important conferences, while he took great pleasure in the visits of friends who came to consult with him here.

At the coming of the winter, we visited San Antonio. Surely it is true that "Southern souls grow responsive in this atmosphere," for father's friends, numberless, were untiring in their devotion. The faithful nurse who was with us in Boerne remained with us here.

During one of the wakeful nights of his illness, a number of friends sat with him— talking politics. Cautioning the men not to let father know of my nightly vigils, in order to prevent his anxiety over my broken rest, I sat quietly at the back of the house.

The night was beautiful—the moon never shone more gloriously. Awakening from a short sleep, father insisted that the night's radiance was the coming of the day. The men could not convince him that it was the moonlight. He lay quiet for a moment and then said in a tender voice;—"If 'Dolly' said that was moonlight, I would know it was true." The men told him; —"Miss Maud is awake. Ask her." I had overheard the conversation and entered the room. He showed no surprise on discovering that I was staying up all night. I think he knew I suffered with him. In his droll way he said, "The boys are lying to me, Dolly; see how bright it is; isn't it daylight?" At my reply, he laughingly asked the men's pardon for disputing them, saying, "I was wrong, fellows; it is moonlight." And then for long, he commented on the beauty of the night.

The next day my Uncle Joseph came from Galveston with my brother and grandmother. It was the third of March.

Members of the family were constantly at his bedside, but wishing to spare his aged mother the heartrending sorrow of his closing hours, father asked that we lead her from the room.

With the most remarkable control of his mental powers, father asked if the papers had come, and from them I was forced with tear-blinded eyes, to read the latest reports of world affairs. It was but a few hours before his death. Thinking that I would forget, he asked me to make a memorandum of those newspapers that had given bulletins of his condition—the Galveston-Dallas

News, San Antonio Express, St. Louis *Globe-Democrat,* and the New York *Press*—that they might have proper notification of his passing away, and then further directed me in the care of personal matters.

Quietly he lay for a few moments, with his head pillowed on my arm.

He whispered, "My work is ended"—a last farewell to the world and, drawing my face down to his, he kissed me good-bye.

The brave, generous heart beat no longer.

My father lay dead.

CHAPTER XXI.

The Last Rites.

When the message of father's death reached Congressman Hawley at Washington, he said— "I never knew a man in whose breast there lived a more earnest and unfaltering love of country. In political contention he was a partisan, bitter sometimes, uncompromising always, but, above it all, he stood for justice. His friends were legion, their cause was his, and wherever he was enlisted, all men knew he would steadfastly remain. He never wavered, he never lowered his flag, and this was the glory of the life that passed to-night at San Antonio."

All day Friday, the 4th of March, at St. Paul M. E. Church in San Antonio, the remains were held in state. Through the thoughtfulness of Hon. R. B. Hawley and Mr. Lee, Collector of Customs at Galveston, the Southern Pacific and the Santa Fe Railroads, in honor to our dead, placed at my service a special train, draped in mourning, which bore the remains, accompanied by members of the family and intimate friends, to our Galveston home.

By permission of Adjutant-General Mabry
of Texas, a guard of honor, the San Antonio
Guards—a colored militia regiment—under the
command of Capt. R. G. Ellis and the direction
of Mr. Richard W. Wallace, acted as escort.

My wishes for quiet ceremonies could not be
fulfilled. Father had lived a life of public service, and it was fitting that the last opportunity
for the people he loved to do him honor, should
not be denied.

Funeral services were held on March 6th at
Galveston. Notices from the Galveston daily
press read: "All that was mortal of N. Wright
Cuney, the Negro politician and leader of his
race, was laid to rest in beautiful Lake View
Cemetery this afternoon. The procession that
followed the body to the grave was the largest
seen in Galveston in many a day. Whites, as
well as blacks, joined in paying a tribute of
respect to the dead leader.

"There thousand people, and quite a number
of leading white citizens, gathered in Harmony
Hall to witness the ceremonies. Perhaps a
thousand people could not gain admission and
remained outside. At 12.30, the remains were
brought from Reedy Chapel where they had lain
in state since their arrival from San Antonio.

"It was after 1 o'clock when the religious services began. Dr. L. H. Reynolds of New Orleans,
assisted by Rev. M. R. Moody, pastor of Reedy

Chapel, conducted the exercises, which were impressive to a degree.

"The Masonic service was conducted by Grand Master J. W. McKinney of Sherman, assisted by Deputy Grand Master Lawrence, and Past Grand Masters Allen and Armstrong. Mr. Wilford H. Smith of New York delivered a eulogy on behalf of the masonic fraternity. Music was rendered by the Reedy Chapel quartette."

The order of the funeral procession was as follows:

Mounted Police
Band
Officiating Ministers

Military companies;
Excelsior Guards of San Antonio,
Cocke Rifles of Houston
Lincoln Guards of Galveston

Civic Societies; Cotton Screwmen No. 2
Longshoremen's Aid Association
Knights of Pythias
Odd Fellows
Masons

Silver Trowell No. 47 of Houston
Magnolia No. 3 of Houston
South Gate No. 32
Amity No. 4
Grand Lodge

Honorary Pall-bearers: W. R. Wallace, I. H.
Tanner, H. G. Williams, and H. E. Ellis of San
Antonio, Webster Wilson, Henry Bee, Dr. J. H.
Wilkins, J. H. Holland, James Blair, J. H. Pat-
rick, Priest Henderson, W. R. Hill, Arthur
Shephard, C. J. Williams, Frank Armand, Lewis
Johnson, William Lane, Albert Piner, Wm.
Holmes, Bailey Sparks of Houston, Jos. Scott,
T. H. Thomas, A. B. Trowell, Prof. John R.
Gibson, W. D. Donnell, W. H. Smith and Alex.
Green.

Active Masonic Pall-bearers: Past Masters
George W. Neviells, John DeBruhl, W. H. Love,
Masters E. M. Russell, H. P. Whittlesey and
Lawrence Cletheral.

One hundred carriages.

The interment was in the family lot at Lake
View Cemetery.

Messages of condolence poured in upon us from
men of distinction all over the country, while
throughout the State political organizations,
charitable and religious societies held memorials
and in their resolutions testified their recognition
of a life so unselfishly and sincerely lived.

Among the many comments on father's ability
as a business man, a politician and a leader, none
gave a truer estimate of the man than those that
follow.   Hon. R. L. Fulton, Mayor of Galveston,
wrote of father in 1889;—"During the past
twenty years that I have known Mr. Cuney as a

public man, he has exercised a remarkable influence on the politics of this city, and invariably in the interests of sound money and honest government.

"In State and National politics, his position and prominence are simply matters of current history to which his Republican friends point with pride, both here and elsewhere, but which, as a Democrat, I have always antagonized to the best of my ability.

"In 1875, Mr. Cuney was nominated by the Republican party of this city, as a candidate for Mayor of Galveston and I had the satisfaction, as the nominee of the Democratic party, of defeating him for that position, and at the same time, of learning of some of his excellent qualities as a public man."

Senator Stephen B. Elkins said of him:—"I have known Mr. Cuney for many years and have always found him manly and honorable. Of his character and standing, I have yet to find a man from Texas or the Southwest who does not speak in the highest terms of him. He enjoys the confidence and respect of both political parties."

Following father's death, Hon. E. H. R. Green wrote me;—"The death of your father is the loss of the greatest leader of his race."

Mr. Thos. Fortune of New York said of him; —"In many respects, N. W. Cuney was the greatest political organizer and manager the Afro-American race has produced; assuredly he was one of the most generous and courageous and at the time of his death no man of his race was known and trusted and loved by more of the national leaders of the Republican party than he. For years he had been a member of the national committee, and honesty had commended him to the good esteem of the men who have dominated the political destinies since the war.

"Mr. Cuney occupied a unique place in the life of Texas. In the winter of 1896, I spent a few months in Texas and was his guest at Galveston and saw much of him.

"In a State where race prejudice is almost as strong as it is in Georgia, he was treated almost everywhere, in places of public amusement and accomodation, as white men are treated. On one occasion we rode out to the Surf House, a very aristocratic resort, and spent a half hour there. His advent in the café attracted the attention of all the people there, people prominent in the varied life of Galveston, who accosted him with the heartiness and courtesy of tried and true comradeship.

"Off in a corner, a stranger, a southerner, much surprised asked his companion;—'Who is that yellow fellow'? 'Oh, that's Wright Cuney,' said in a way to settle the Black Flagger's right

in the place. 'Indeed! I have heard lots of him.
He looks like a Mexican and as fierce as one.'
'Oh, Wright Cuney can take care of himself.'
So he could; and that was the general opinion
all over Texas. 'That's Wright Cuney,' was
sufficient to give him a right of way where other
men of his race would have been thrust out without ceremony or mobbed, not because he resembled a Mexican, but because he had brains
and courage and had won the leadership of a
great party by hard knocks and steady blows,
and was a gentleman of the true southern type,
generous and impulsive, so that all Texans of all
races and colors were proud of him and
respected him.

"The devotion of the Afro-American race of
Texas to Mr. Cuney was one of the strongest
and strangest in our politics and was such as no
other man of his race has ever enjoyed in this
country. In most southern states, actual leadership has been vested in white men. Florida,
Georgia and Louisiana have been exceptions to
the rule and Mississippi is now; but in none of
those states did the black voters stick as closely
to a black leader as those of Texas did to Norris
Wright Cuney."

Mr. Wm. H. McDonald of Fort Worth, Texas,
says of him:—"The Negro race looked for and
needed a man worthy to lead them—looked for
a man who was a ripe student, who had the

audacity of genius and was a good combination
of heart, conscience and brain.　Mr. N. W.
Cuney, the gallant 'Yellow Rose' of Galveston
County—this political leader with patriotism as
taintless as the air, battled for the rights of
others.　He fought his political battles to prevent arrogance from predominating over his
patient brethren, and the women and children
of his race.　This man stands alone—ancient or
modern degeneracy did not reach him.

"The white Republicans thought his high
standing in political fields so impaired theirs,
that they conspired to remove him in order to be
relieved of his superiority.

"No State chicanery, no narrow system of
vicious politics, no idle contest for ministerial
victories sank him to the vulgar level of the
great men of the race; his object was advance,
his ambition, race pride and patriotism.

"Without appealing to race, he destroyed his
party enemies; without corruption, he ruled the
Republican party of Texas.　His idea was to
make a venal age glorious.

"The ordinary feelings which made life
amiable and indolent—those sensations which
soften, allure and vulgarize were unknown to
him.　Aloof from the sordid occurrences of life
and unsullied by its intercourse, he came into
our system to counsel and decide.　A character
so exalted, so strenuous, so authoritative, aston-

ished corrupt politicians and a corrupt age, and they all trembled at the name of Cuney.

"Nothing can be said that would add a single laurel or ray of glory to the chaplet of fame bound about his brow by the willing hands of a loving people. Words are futile to express the unbounded admiration of his people, in which their confidence and love encompass him."

In his eulogy, Dr. Reynolds said;—"Life was not to him a holiday, a thing to be enjoyed with song and laughter and tinsel and glitter, but it was the sphere and opportunity for stern, uncompromising, unrelenting conflict with adverse conditions and hostile forces.

"He was courageous. N. W. Cuney was no trimmer. What he believed he held to with the tenacity of a great and vigorous mind, and then had the courage to proclaim it when others fled or were discreetly silent. This spectacle was often seen in his stormy career, in conference, in conventions, on the hustings, the masses spurred on by short-sighted leaders and burning with misdirected zeal bent in one direction, and this man often single-handed and alone standing before them, his massive brow furrowed with lines of determination, his eyes ablaze, his outstretched hand pointing the right way and his voice sounding above the roar of discontent. 'You shall go this way,' and they went his way.

"He was a born leader of men. The ability

to plan wisely and then to project those plans into the minds of others with such clearness and force as to secure approval, is no mean power. It is the basis upon which has rested the success of the world's great leaders.

"He was a resourceful man. No one ever knew when he was defeated. Often when in the heat of battle some one sounded retreat, when disaster seemed traced in letters of ominous blackness on the banner which floated over his scattered allies, he would emerge at the head of a new force and move on to victory.

"He was an intense race man. He thought and planned and hoped and fought for his race. Because of his superior intelligence and the respect in which he was held everywhere, even among the most cultured of the land, he might have drifted away from his people, as many have done but, like Moses of old, he chose rather to suffer affliction with his own people than to enjoy honors and pleasure with another race.

" 'Know ye not that a great man has fallen this day in Israel.' "

THE END.

ABOUT THE EDITORS

Henry Louis Gates, Jr., is the W. E. B. Du Bois Professor of the Humanities, Chair of the Afro-American Studies Department, and Director of the W. E. B. Du Bois Institute for Afro-American Research at Harvard University. One of the leading scholars of African-American literature and culture, he is the author of *Figures in Black: Words, Signs, and the Racial Self* (1987), *The Signifying Monkey: A Theory of Afro-American Literary Criticism* (1988), *Loose Canons: Notes on the Culture Wars* (1992), and the memoir *Colored People* (1994).

Jennifer Burton is in the Ph.D. program in English Language and Literature at Harvard University. She is the volume editor of *The Prize Plays and Other One-Acts* in this series. She was a contributor to *Great Lives from History: American Women*, and, with her mother and sister, coauthored two one-act plays, *Rita's Haircut* and *Litany of the Clothes*. Her creative non-fiction has appeared in *There and Back* and *Buffalo*, the Sunday magazine of the *Buffalo News*.

Tera W. Hunter is Assistant Professor of History at the University of North Carolina, Chapel Hill. Her writings on African-American history and culture have appeared in *Labor History*, *Callaloo*, and *Southern Exposure*.